Grillin', Chillin', and Swillin'

(or How a Technology Geek Cooked His Way Through Unemployment)

Bill Allen

authorHOUSE®

AuthorHouse™
1663 Liberty Drive
Bloomington, IN 47403
www.authorhouse.com
Phone: 1-800-839-8640

First published by AuthorHouse   12/22/2010

ISBN: 978-1-4567-1351-5 (sc)
ISBN: 978-1-4567-1775-9 (e)

Library of Congress Control Number: 2010918650

Printed in the United States of America

Any people depicted in stock imagery provided by Thinkstock are models,
and such images are being used for illustrative purposes only.
Certain stock imagery © Thinkstock.

This book is printed on acid-free paper.

Author photo by Laura Crawford

For Marcie, who still cooks much better than I do

Contents

Do you look at a menu and say, "Okay"?
- Rodney Dangerfield in "Back to School"

Introduction

For the last twenty-five years, I have worked all over the world as an Information Technology Consultant in the banking industry. You, perhaps, may think that would make me one of the least qualified people in the world to write a cookbook; however, keep in mind that I've been pretty fond of eating during this time. In fact, I *love* food. I love everything about it – everything from the color of an orange Habanero pepper to the texture of a properly cooked Bolognese to the smell of garlic and onions being sautéed. (Oh boy, I knew this would happen. I have to stop writing now and go have a sandwich!)

My travel opportunities have allowed me to see exciting places, meet many wonderful friends, and eventually meet Marcie who I finally talked into marrying me. If that weren't enough, it also gave me the opportunity to enjoy foods that I might never have otherwise heard of, let alone taste; foods like Slovak beef and onion-filled potato pancakes Tatra Mountain style and Huachinango Veracruzana (red snapper Vera Cruz, Mexico style).

Over the years, my passion for food has grown in almost direct proportion with my waistline. The exception to this stunning mathematical equation is the fact that whenever I've been able to drop a few pounds, my love of food has never been questioned.

For many years, my career flowed from one project to the next, my life from one menu and wine list to another. Then the unexpected happened. I was working on a banking project that was suddenly put on "permanent hold" due to the merger of my client with another bank. I'm pretty sure that this is some new, politically correct way of saying that my project had been cancelled. As a consultant, this was not something that I considered to be good news. Marcie didn't think so either. With our impending nuptials less than three months away and no immediate job offers on the horizon, I took the position of *Chef de Cuisine de la Casa y Control de Perro* (cooking at home and dog walking).

Through this period of job hunting, cooking, and dog walking, Marcie suggested that I record my recipes and perhaps tell some stories about them. She also suggested that it would be a good idea to get my recipes on paper for my sons in case my life of leisure resulted in memory loss due to too many extended happy hours. You know - something to do during the day so that I didn't drive both of us insane with all of the free time and nervous energy that I had. After all, it's just not right to start cocktail hour at 3pm *every* day.

Let's eat!

Beginnings

I wasn't always a computer guy. A few weeks after my fifteenth birthday, I got a job as a busboy with a small family-style restaurant chain in my hometown of Homestead, Florida. Actually, my grandfather, who was the maintenance man for the restaurant chain, got me the job. Realizing my vast potential in the kitchen, I was promoted to dishwasher after only 3 or 4 months. I learned a number of things working this first job – the exhilaration of earning a first paycheck, lessons about teamwork, and, most importantly, the mysterious chemical bonding reaction that takes place in 3 hours between country style gravy and a saucepot rendering the two virtually inseparable.

My next job was in South Carolina in a similar type restaurant. My dad, also a technology geek, had changed jobs and moved the family in what was to become a semi-regular pattern for several years. I was still fifteen years old at the time and, because of the laws in South Carolina, my mom had to come to the interview with me. Full of confidence after six months of real restaurant experience (and advanced industry related chemistry studies), I was ready for the ultimate interview question from Joel, the General Manager of the local Shoney's Big Boy.

"Who is always right?"

"The boss," I responded without hesitation.

"It's actually the customer, but you'll do just fine," Joel replied.

I eventually talked my way into a waiter position at Shoney's, but not before validating one of life's most important truths, perhaps better known as Allen's 1st Rule of Chemistry. This rule states that the intensity with which burned on country style gravy sticks to a pot is constant irrespective of the southern state in which the gravy is cooked.

Waiting tables was a blast. It's a very simple concept really. Dudley Moore compared waiters to Santa Claus in the movie *Arthur*. He said, "Waiters are great. You ask them for things and they bring them to you. Kind of like Santa Claus." (See, it's true. I wasn't just shamelessly name-dropping).

After trying my hand at other high school vocations like skating rink floor guard and minor rock star, the family moved to the bustling metropolis of Columbia, South Carolina, before the start of my final semester of high school. I've often thought of this as an example (or you may say rationalization) of why I've never been good at putting down roots. By the time I graduated high school, I had attended 13 schools. Avocado Elementary, Colonial Christian, West Homestead, Neva King Cooper, Homestead Jr. High, Campbell Drive Jr. High, Rawlinson Road Jr. High, Northwestern High, South Dade High, Northwestern (again), York High, Northwestern (a third time), and Columbia High. (See, I wasn't just shamelessly "school-number dropping".) I have the unique perspective of not really knowing a soul from the high school from which I graduated. I remember two fellow students only because they worked in a restaurant in Columbia with me.

In Columbia, we lived around the corner from a fairly high-end restaurant called The Chopping Block: prime rib, lobster, and king crab – typical upscale fare. My dad often took the family there for dinner. It was quite a different experience for me because, the first time we came for dinner, I didn't see a drive-thru window. Dad became friends with the manager of the dining room and this was instrumental in me being offered a job. As I wasn't yet eighteen years old, and therefore not allowed to serve alcohol, I took a job doing prep work in the afternoons and busboy work in the evenings. In addition to vacuuming the entire restaurant daily, I finally got to work with food other than the uneaten remnants of someone else's dirty plate. Cutting bread and lemons, clarifying butter, and even (occasionally) getting to make sautéed mushrooms were part of the deal.

After high school, I bounced around some more between minor rock star (redux), skating rink deejay, pizza and sub sandwich place, and cooking in a fried chicken joint. The important thing to remember here, I kept telling myself, was that I always had a job.

Finding myself once again in south Florida, I took a job at a family owned diner as a cook. My grandfather was a friend of the owners. (Perhaps if my grandparents had been friends with Frank Sinatra instead of restaurant owners, my music career would have been more successful.) At any rate, this was the perfect job for a nineteen year old. I worked every other day, 13 hours per shift, and every other Sunday. This meant that I cooked breakfast, lunch, and dinner. Even though it was a fairly low volume place, one had to know all of the dishes and preparations. Did I mention that the owners, like my grandfather, were Italians? It's funny, thinking back, that the only thing this restaurant served that I have adapted and continued to make is a steak sandwich. Having said that, they also taught me to flip eggs and run a kitchen efficiently. Unfortunately, there was no country style gravy on the menu, so I couldn't revalidate Allen's 1st Rule of Chemistry.

The next stop on my tour of kitchens and dining rooms was a Florida steakhouse where I finally got to cook over an open flame. There is nothing quite like keeping track of 30 steaks grilling at the same time, monitoring the temperature of each, and making it through an entire evening of service without a single order being sent back to the kitchen. It was here also that I learned how to cut meat and manage a restaurant. Subsequently, I cut at two other steak houses over the years, but I'll always remember the Longhorn Steak House in Homestead for a couple of reasons. One of them is that there are not many experiences that compare to a boy and his first grill.

I've worked intermittently at other restaurants over the years, mostly waiting tables and doing a little bartending to pick up extra money. Whether upscale or not, these restaurants all gave me a renewed perspective of the common connection that we as people share and restaurants by extension bring to light – people love to eat and drink and share life over cocktails and dinner.

Appetizers

Ahhh… appetizers. Call them what you will – starters, entradas, tapas, antipasti – appetizers are often the best part of the meal. When you think about it, the entire "small plate" craze is based on the appetizer-sized portion. Just enough to whet the appetite and leave it begging for more. Marcie and I have found that, in many places, the starters have been our favorite part of dining out. Because of this, we frequently forego main courses in favor of sharing 4 or 5 starters.

Another reason that we're appetizer whores is because we love to entertain. This is not to say that we only serve apps at dinner parties. Quite the contrary; but for smaller gatherings, good appetizers can distinguish you as a host who puts more thought and effort into his or her party menu. Better yet, most apps are relatively easy to make and don't have to be cost prohibitive to serve.

One idea that we like to employ when we cook for parties is to deconstruct a main course dish into an appetizer and adjust the portion size accordingly. It's also a cost-effective way for an unemployed techno-geek to be able to eat on a regular basis. A number of the recipes that I include in this chapter are simply scaled down versions of an entrée. This is the approach that I took when Marcie threw down the gauntlet on the "Small Plate Challenge."

The Small Plate Challenge came about one evening when we were sitting at home, watching cooking shows, and unable to decide what we would make for dinner. Since deciding where to go or what to make for dinner can be one of the greatest sources of stress in our relationship, we've turned evenings like this into a game. The conversation usually goes something like this….

"So what would you like for me to make you for dinner," I ask.

"Oh, Honey, I don't know," Marcie replies.

"Well, it's 5:30pm, so we should probably decide soon so that I can thaw something out or go to the store if I need to," I'll say. "'The Biggest Loser' comes on at 8:00 and you know how we like to eat dinner while we watch it!"

"I'd be happy to just have popcorn," she says.

"I know, but we should probably cook something else just in case the popcorn isn't enough," I'll continue.

"I don't know, why don't you decide," she'll say.

"Okay, how about tacos?" I'll ask.

"Uh, no, I don't want tacos," she'll answer.

"Then, what about fish?"

"We've already had fish three times this week. I need a day off from fish."

Invariably, the I/T project management guy in me will start coming out at this point in the conversation. Since we don't have time to create a Microsoft Project plan to enter and track everything that we've eaten in the last two weeks and still have time to have dinner before midnight, I'll say something like, "Okay, this is becoming too complicated. How about we narrow dinner down to a particular continent, then to a specific country within the continent, then to a particular type of food."

"Fine. Which continent gets credit for popcorn," Marcie asks.

"How about we eliminate continents, then countries until we have one country left?" I say.

"Okay," she replies. "I eliminate South America."

"I'll eliminate Africa, then," I reply.

"Antarctica"

"Australia."

"North America."

"Asia."

"Well, it looks like we're left with Europe," Marcie says.

"Okay, I'll get rid of the Ukraine," I say.

"Is Uzbekistan in Europe?" she asks.

"I think it's in Asia," I respond.

"Could we just agree to have tapas?"

"Do I have to do everything Spanish-style?" I ask.

"No, just small portions," she says.

"How about this?" I ask. "What if I take a fixed amount of money, go to the store, and come back and make several different tapas?"

"Here's forty dollars," Marcie says. "You have to stay under budget and be back here thirty minutes from…ready…. *OKAY, NOW*!"

Fortunately, there is a grocery store about a mile away from our home. I was gone and back in twenty-eight minutes and still had $4.67 in change. Over the next two hours, I prepared and we shared five courses of tapas and two bottles of wine. We started with Tequila Lime Chicken Livers, moved on to "Ocean 3 Ways", then tried bacon wrapped scallops seared in a tiny bit of port next, progressed to lamb with miniature roasted potatoes, and finished with beef with a black peppercorn and red zinfandel reduction.

"What about dessert?" Marcie asked.

"Wine seems like a good dessert to me," I replied, exhausted.

Mini Italian Sausages

This is a variation on a New Year's Eve tradition at my grandparents' house that my mother still makes every Christmas Eve. For many years, I did a full-blown Christmas Eve sit-down Italian dinner at home for over 20 people. As I often use Italian sausage in my red sauce, it's always been a little treat for the chef to cut a sausage in half and put it on half of a hotdog bun with some of the sauce and some shredded Parmesan cheese on top. For a typical party, and no red sauce splatter, I make them a little easier to handle. By twisting the individual sausage links in half, without breaking the casing, then cutting at the twisted point in the center, you'll wind up with 2 appetizer-sized sausages from each of the links. This recipe yields 10 mini sausages and even though this sounds like "man food," we've found that our female guests enjoy this dish as much as the guys do.

For Turnin' and Burnin'

1 Large Pot

1 Charcoal or Gas grill

Cutting Board

Grill Tongs

1 Cheese Grater

1 Bottle Opener for the beer

Ingredients

5 tbsp. olive oil
5 mild or hot Italian sausage links, twisted and cut in half as described above
1 large onion, peeled and halved, one half chopped
3 whole cloves garlic, peeled
5 – 6 inch Italian sub rolls cut in half
4 oz. roughly grated Asiago or Parmesan cheese
Stone ground or brown mustard.

To Swill while you Grill

Moretti (Italian Beer). Any other beer will do nicely as well!

Preparation

- Bring 3 quarts of water to a boil in a large pot.
- Add the 2 tbsp of olive oil, the unchopped half onion, garlic, half of the beer and sausage.
- Parboil the sausages for 20 minutes.
- While parboiling the sausages, preheat outdoor grill to 300 degrees.
- Once sausages have parboiled, remove from heat, and place on the grill.
- Feel free to drink the other half of the beer at this time. The sausages have cooked through by this point; we're just putting a nice browning and some grill marks on them. This is why we have outdoor grills – so we can cook sausages and drink beer.
- Be sure to turn the sausages often to prevent them from over-charring.
- Coat the inside of the buns with the other 3 tbsp. of olive oil and cook coated side down until gently browned.
- Place 1 mini sausage on each bun.
- Serve with the chopped onions, grated cheese, and mustard on the side.

Pico de Gallo

This is an incredibly easy recipe that goes with so many dishes. I've used it in everything from a Mexican style shrimp sauté to topping breakfast burritos with it. In the winter, we're fortunate to have a Saturday morning vegetable market where we can get everything fresh for this recipe except for the salt and pepper.

For Turnin' and Burnin'

Chef's Knife
Cutting Board
Large Mixing Bowl
Margarita Glass

Ingredients

3 large ripe tomatoes, seeded and chopped into ½ inch cubes
1 large onion or 10 small spring onions, chopped into ¼ inch pieces (or sliced into fine rings if using spring onions)
1 Cubanelle pepper, seeded and chopped into ¼ inch pieces
2 Jalapeno or Serrano peppers, seeded and chopped into ¼ inch pieces
Juice of 1 lime
3 tbsp. cilantro, finely chopped
Sea salt to taste
Black pepper to taste

To Swill while you Chill

I advise against tequila shots while doing large amounts of chopping. A Margarita is a nice alternative.

Preparation

- Combine tomatoes, onions, and peppers into a large bowl and mix thoroughly.
- Add the lime juice, salt, and pepper and mix again.
- Add cilantro, stirring once more.
- Chill for 30 minutes.
- Transfer to a serving bowl, stir, and serve with tortilla chips.

Strawberry-Papaya Salsa

For a sweet alternative to Pico, fruit salsas are quite popular. I like to experiment with different combinations of fruits and chilis. Substitute mangoes, pineapples, or other fresh fruit in season. The sweetness of the fruit contrasted with the heat from the chilis pair especially nicely with breakfast dishes, grilled fish and pork dishes.

For Turnin' and Burnin'

Chef's Knife
Cutting Board
Large Mixing Bowl
Champagne Flute

Ingredients

½ cup fresh strawberries (stems removed), chopped
½ cup fresh papaya, peeled and chopped
Juice of lime
2 Serrano peppers, seeded and finely diced
3 tbsp. cilantro, finely chopped
½ tsp. black pepper

To Swill while you Chill

Float a piece of chopped strawberry in a glass of champagne and enjoy while realizing how fortunate you are to have access to fresh fruit like papayas.

Preparation

- Combine strawberries and papayas in a large bowl and mix thoroughly.
- Add the lime juice and pepper and mix again.
- Add cilantro, stirring once more.
- Chill for 15 minutes.
- Transfer to a serving bowl to serve or spoon over entrees.

Guacamole

As far as I can tell, guacamole is the reason that God made avocados. When making "guac" in the traditional fashion, the avocados are mashed by hand. For speed and ease, I normally pulse the avocados in a food processor. If you choose to use a food processor, be careful to pulse-cut the avocados; otherwise you'll turn your guacamole into avocado soup.

Guacamole, much like Pico de Gallo, is a super garnish for Mexican dishes but also makes a great appetizer when served with tortilla chips.

For Turnin' and Burnin'

Chef's Knife
Cutting Board
Measuring Cup
Measuring Spoon
Food Processor
Shot Glass

Ingredients

1 medium tomato, seeded and diced
2 avocados, peeled, seeded, and roughly chopped
¼ cup onion, chopped
2 tbsp. cilantro leaves
½ tsp. garlic powder
½ tsp. ground cumin
2 Jalapeno or Serrano peppers, seeded and chopped into ¼ inch pieces
1 tbsp. Tabasco
Juice of 1 Lime
Sea salt to taste
Black pepper to taste

To Swill while you Chill

Okay, go ahead and have that tequila shot – just be sure not to cut yourself while using the food processor.

Preparation
- Combine all ingredients in a food processor and pulse until avocados are chopped.
- Adjust salt, pepper, and hot sauce to taste and serve with tortilla chips.

Kalamata Olive Tapenade

Other than grape flavored "SweeTarts", Kalamata Olive Tapenade is my favorite purple food. If you like your Tapenade less salty, omit the anchovy filet. Spread this inside of pita pockets and fill with roasted lamb for a tasty alternative to a sandwich.

For Turnin' and Burnin'
Chef's Knife
Cutting Board
Measuring Cup
Measuring Spoon
Food Processor
Old Fashioned Glass

Ingredients
1 cup Kalamata olives, pitted
¼ cup pine nuts
¼ cup olive oil
Juice of 1 lemon
1 garlic clove, peeled
1 tbsp. capers
1 anchovy filet (optional)
1 tsp. fresh thyme
1 tsp. black pepper, ground

To Swill while you Chill
Ouzo is the obvious suggestion, right? Try a Bouzo (pronounced BOOZE-oh) instead. Here's what you do. Pour 2 oz of bourbon in an Old Fashioned glass, and then pour an ounce of ouzo on top of it. Think of it as "Jack Daniel meets Aristotle."

Preparation
- Combine olives, pine nuts, garlic, capers, anchovies, thyme, and lemon juice in a food processor and pulse until all ingredients are well chopped.
- Slowly add the olive oil and pulse to combine with other ingredients.
- Add black pepper to taste and serve with crackers or pita bread.

Pluots and Gorgonzola Wrapped in Prosciutto

Pluots are a complex hybrid of a plum and an apricot developed in the 20th century by Floyd Zaiger. You can substitute a number of different things for the pluots if you like. I first prepared this recipe with fresh figs, and then did a variation with dates. I've also made the dish using shrimp instead of fruit, all with very tasty results. Originally, I would wrap the Prosciutto around the fruit or shrimp, broil, then top with the cheese and continue broiling until the cheese melted. It tasted fine but made a heck of a mess, as the cheese wanted to fall off of the Prosciutto. I finally settled on putting the cheese inside of the wrapped Prosciutto and cooking the whole thing together. Easier to handle, less mess.

For Turnin' and Burnin'
Butcher's Knife
Cutting Board
Cookie Sheet
Wine Glass

Ingredients
6 oz. thinly sliced Prosciutto de Parma
4 Pluots, peeled with pit removed, and sliced into ¼ inch by 1 inch pieces
4 oz. Gorgonzola cheese, softened
2 sprigs fresh rosemary
16 toothpicks

To Swill while you Grill
You know that you're going to taste the leftover pluots while you're putting this together. Pinot Grigio will pair nicely with the fruit.

Preparation
- Preheat the oven to Broil.
- Slice the Prosciutto in half width-wise.
- Near one end of each slice of Prosciutto, place a pluot slice and a small dollop of Gorgonzola.
- Wrap the Prosciutto around the cheese and fruit and roll completely.
- Broil on a cookie sheet for 2 minutes on each side.
- Arrange on a serving platter with the rosemary, place a toothpick into each roll and serve immediately.

Mini Shrimp Quesadillas
Like their name suggests, these are appetizer versions of their bigger siblings. You can make the quesadillas whatever size you like, and grill or brown them on the stovetop. I prefer making them 2 ½ to 3 inches in diameter and cooking the assembled product on a Panini press. Make sure that you use ripe avocado to avoid any bitterness in flavor. The recipe below calls for Pico de Gallo. If you'd like to try a fruitier twist, try substituting Mango Salsa for the Pico.

For Turnin' and Burnin'
3 inch Cookie Cutter
Cutting Board
Grill Brush
Spatula
Panini Press or large Frying Pan
Bottle Opener for the beer

Ingredients
2 tbsp. olive oil
12 medium shrimp, peeled, deveined and sliced lengthwise in half.
4 – 10 inch flour tortillas
4 - ¼ inch thick slices of avocado, cut into thirds
½ cup Pico de Gallo
4 oz. shredded sharp cheddar cheese

To Swill while you Grill
You're going to be flipping 24 mini quesadillas so you don't want to have to worry about breaking a wine glass. Drink a Mexican beer like Pacifico straight from the bottle as you display your Panini grilling prowess.

Preparation
- Preheat the Panini press to 350 degrees.
- Using a 3 inch cookie cutter, cut mini tortillas out of each large tortilla. You should be able to get at least 6 minis for each large tortilla.
- Set mini tortillas aside.
- Sautee the Pico and shrimp together, about three minutes or until shrimp is pink and opaque.
- Assemble the Quesadillas by placing 2 of the sliced, cooked shrimp and enough of the Pico to cover a mini tortilla on 12 of the minis.
- Top each with a slice of avocado and sprinkled cheese then cover with a second mini tortilla.
- Brush Olive oil onto the outside of one side of each mini quesadilla and place on the Panini press oil side down.
- Brush oil on the top of the mini quesadilla and cook for 2 minutes on each side or until the quesadillas are golden brown and the cheese has melted.
- Serve hot with Pico or Salsa Verde on the side.

Tequila Lime Shrimp

I believe that anytime you can leverage one recipe into multiple recipes that you're ahead of the game. Such is the case with this Tequila Lime Shrimp recipe. Once I've prepared the Pico de Gallo recipe, most of the work is done. Marinating the shrimp and grilling becomes a snap. The recipe below is for the grilled, appetizer version of the dish; however, doubling the recipe, sautéed and served over rice, this dish also makes a nice entrée. Other variations on this theme that I've enjoyed are using the grilled shrimp skewers as a Bloody Mary garnish or the sautéed shrimp as a topping for Vera Cruz Red Snapper.

For Turnin' and Burnin'
Your Trusty Grill
Grill Tongs
Large Plate for the skewers (to and from the grill)

Ingredients
2 tbsp. olive oil
1 cup Pico de Gallo
¼ cup Tequila
16 medium shrimp, peeled and deveined
1 tsp. freshly cracked black pepper
4 wooden skewers
Bottle opener

To Swill while you Grill
Try adding a little salt and 1 tbsp of fresh lime juice to a glass before filling it with a light Mexican beer like Sol or Corona.

Preparation
- Combine all ingredients (yes, except the skewers) in a large bowl and mix thoroughly.
- Cover and refrigerate for 45 minutes.
- Soak the skewers in cold water for 30 minutes. This will help to prevent the skewers from burning on the grill.
- Preheat grill to 375 degrees.
- Thread 4 shrimp onto each skewer.
- Grill the skewers until the shrimp turn opaque, turning once, about 4 minutes total.
- Serve hot.

Tequila Lime Chicken Livers

I promise that this is the last of the "Tequila Lime" family that I'll share with you. Other than replacing the shrimp with chicken livers and cooking on the stovetop, you'll notice that this recipe is very similar to my Tequila Lime Shrimp.

For Turnin' and Burnin'
Kitchen Tongs
Large Bowl
Large Spoon
Large Sauté Pan
8 Toothpicks
Champagne Flute

Ingredients
2 tbsp. olive oil
1 cup Pico de Gallo
¼ cup Tequila
16 chicken livers, washed
1 tsp. freshly cracked black pepper

To Swill while you Grill
Think "*pâté de poulet*" and have a glass (or two) of the bubbly while concocting this appetizer.

Preparation
- Thread 2 chicken livers onto each of the toothpicks and add to the marinade.
- Add the Pico, tequila, and black peppers to a large mixing bowl.
- Refrigerate for 30 minutes.
- Over medium-high heat on the stovetop, pour the marinade and livers into a large saucepan.
- Sauté for 6 minutes or until the livers are cooked throughout.
- Serve hot.

Stuffed Mushrooms

Stuffed mushrooms make the perfect Amuse Bouche (small bite appetizer). They avail themselves to a number of different fillings and you get the added bonus of being able to eat the vessel in which the stuffing is served. I frequently prepare this recipe using a mixture of crab and shrimp stuffing but can also served as one or the other by doubling up on either the crab or the shrimp. My mom usually makes her stuffed mushrooms using an Italian sausage mixture and they are always a hit. For a party, why not make some of each and enjoy several different versions of this classic?

For Turnin' and Burnin'
Cookie Sheet
Large saucepan
Chef's Knife
Cutting Board
Large Mixing Bowl
Wineglass
Corkscrew

Ingredients
8 oz. button mushrooms, washed and caps removed for each version of the dish that you are preparing.

For the Sausage Stuffing

2 tbsp. olive oil

12 oz. ground Italian sausage, casings removed if present

1 clove garlic, minced

1 tsp. oregano

1 tsp. freshly cracked black pepper

2 tbsp. finely grated Parmesan cheese

For the Seafood Stuffing

6 oz. ground lump crab meat (use 12 oz crab and omit shrimp for a crab only stuffing)

6 oz. diced baby shrimp (use 12 oz shrimp and omit crab for a shrimp only recipe)

1 tsp. fresh thyme, minced

2 tbsp. finely grated bread crumbs

1 tsp. Dijon mustard

2 tbsp. celery, minced

1 tsp. freshly cracked black pepper

2 tbsp. finely shredded Swiss cheese

To Swill while you Grill

If you're only making the seafood stuffed mushrooms, go with an unoaked Chardonnay. If you're only doing the sausage stuffed version, go with a Barbara. If you're making both, drink some of each or split the difference with a Pinot Noir.

Preparation
For the Sausage Stuffing

- Combine the sausage, garlic, oregano, and black pepper in a large bowl and mix thoroughly.
- Over medium high heat, sauté the sausage mixture until browned, about 6 minutes.
- Remove from heat and transfer to a large bowl.

For the Seafood Stuffing

- Combine all ingredients in a large bowl and mix thoroughly.
- Cover and refrigerate for 20 minutes.

To turn all of this into something really tasty,
(Flash back to COBOL Computer Geek days)....

```
*

    SAUSAGE-MUSHROOMS.
    IF NOT PREPARING-SAUSAGE-MUSHROOMS
    GO TO SEAFOOD-MUSHROOMS
    ELSE
    SPOON SAUSAGE MIXTURE INTO MUSHROOMS
```

```
        PLACE MUSHROOMS ON COOKIE SHEET
        TOP WITH PARMESAN CHEESE.
*
        SEAFOOD-MUSHROOMS.
        IF NOT PREPARING-SEAFOOD-MUSHROOMS
        GO TO COOK-MUSHROOMS
        ELSE
        SPOON SAUSAGE MIXTURE INTO MUSHROOMS
        PLACE MUSHROOMS ON COOKIE SHEET
        TOP WITH PARMESAN CHEESE.
*
        COOK-MUSHROOMS
        IF NO-MUSROOMS-ARE-STUFFED
        DISPLAY 'YOU FORGOT TO STUFF THE 'SHROOMS
        GO TO SAUSAGE STUFFING
        ELSE
        PREHEAT OVEN TO 400 DEGREES
        BAKE MUSHROOMS FOR 10 MINUTES
        ARRANGE ON A TRAY
        SERVE
        EAT.
```

For those of you who have no desire to debug my COBOL code, here's what you do:

- Preheat the oven to 400 degrees.
- Carefully spoon whatever type of stuffing you have made into the mushroom caps and place onto a cookie sheet.
- Top the Italian sausage mushrooms with the Parmesan.
- Bake for 10 Minutes.
- Remove from the oven, arrange on a tray, serve and eat.

For those of you who would like to critique my COBOL coding technique, remember, I'm writing for cooks and not the Systems Architecture Review Board, okay. Have a glass of Pinot Noir and continue reading, secure in the knowledge that you just might be a better COBOL coder than I am.

Grilled Provoletta

One of the best reasons to go to an Argentine cookout (or asado) is that grilled Provoletta may be on the menu. If you like provolone cheese, this is an example of **more** definitely being better.

__For Turnin' and Burnin'__
Mixing Bowl
Your trusty Outdoor Grill
Grill Brush
Spatula
Wineglass
Corkscrew

__Ingredients__
¼ cup olive oil
1 tsp. dried oregano
½ tsp. powdered garlic
1 tsp. salt
1 tsp. freshly cracked black pepper
3 – ½ inch thick slices of provolone cheese
3 tomato slices (optional)

__To Swill while you Grill__
Italian cheese (as with any food) should be paired with... whatever you like! However, since it's my job to make recommendations here, I'd go with a glass of Chianti while grilling the provolone.

__Preparation__
- Combine the olive oil with all of the dry ingredients in a small bowl and mix thoroughly.
- Preheat grill to low heat.
- Brush half of the oil mixture on one side of the cheese and place oiled side directly on the grill (or on aluminum foil, if you prefer).
- Brush remaining oil mixture on the top of the cheese.
- Grill until the bottom side begins to soften and begins to melt.
- Carefully turn, and repeat for other side.
- If planning to top with tomatoes, dip the tomato slices into the oil and herb marinade and briefly grill over low heat. Place a tomato slice on top of each piece of cheese.
- Remove from heat.
- Slice into wedges and serve with Chimichurri and fresh bread.

Shrimp 'n Crab Cakes

Here's another appetizer that can double as an entrée. The base ingredients of this recipe (minus the egg) double as the stuffing for my Crab and Shrimp Stuffed Tilapia. For a traditional crab cake, replace the shrimp with 6 additional ounces of crab. I employ a "pan-to-oven-to-pan" technique in order to ensure a crisp crust on the cakes. Serve with Sauvignon Blanc or Chardonnay.

Bill Allen

For Turnin' and Burnin'
12" Sauté Pan
Large Rubber Spoon
Large Mixing Bowl
Cutting Board
Chef's Knife
Measuring Cup
Measuring Spoons
3-inch Cookie Cutter
Baking Dish
Wineglass
Corkscrew

Ingredients
3 tbsp. olive oil
6 oz. white crab meat
8 shrimp, washed, deveined, and diced
2 spring onions, diced
1 celery stick, diced
1 jalapeño, diced
2 tsp. fresh thyme
2 tbsp. prepared horseradish
1 egg, beaten
¼ cup dry white wine (like Chardonnay or Sauvignon Blanc)
¼ cup cream cheese, at room temperature
4 tbsp Panko bread crumbs
Juice of 2 limes
Kosher salt
Black pepper

To Swill while you Grill
In the recipe description and in the ingredient list, I've indicated that either a Chardonnay or Sauvignon Blanc would be a good idea. What? Don't you believe me? That's okay. As another option for those who don't care for white wine, try a vodka and club soda with a splash of cranberry juice and a twist of lime.

Preparation
- Over medium-high heat, add 2 tbsp of the olive oil to a 12" sauté pan.
- Add the onions, celery, and jalapeños, heating and gently stirring until the onions are translucent, about 3 minutes.
- Add the crab, shrimp, thyme, and white wine and continue sautéing for 4 minutes more.
- Add salt and pepper to taste.
- Remove crab/shrimp mixture from heat and transfer to a mixing bowl.

- Add 2 tbsp of the breadcrumbs, the horseradish, egg, and cream cheese and stir until thoroughly combined.
- Use a 3-inch cookie cutter to shape the cakes, then refrigerate on a plate for 1 hour.
- Preheat oven to 400 degrees.
- Carefully press remaining breadcrumbs onto top and bottom of each cake.
- Place cakes on a baking dish and bake for 15 minutes.
- Heat remaining olive in the 12" sauté pan.
- Remove cakes from oven and transfer to the sauté pan.
- Cook for 1-2 minutes per side until crust is browned and crispy.
- Serve hot.

Butter and Parmesan Grilled Oysters

Get out your oyster knife and fire up the grill. For a way-cool seductive appetizer, this combination has very few equals. Paired with Champagne, I can think of no better starter for a romantic evening. I've proportioned this recipe to serve two people. (You wouldn't want to start getting too romantic with other people around!)

For Turnin' and Burnin'
Your best friend, Mr. Grill
Oyster Knife
Measuring Cup
Measuring Spoons
Champagne Flutes

Ingredients
1 dozen oysters, thoroughly washed and brushed; shucked
4 tbsp. butter
Juice of 1 lemon
1 cup Parmesan cheese

To Swill while you Grill
Champagne or sparkling wine is my choice for before, during, and after the oysters.

Preparation
- Pour two glasses of champagne sparking wine and enjoy them with someone you love (or really like) while you preheat the grill to a high heat. If you're alone, drink both glasses. It's okay, you're worth it!
- Place the oysters on a hot grill, shell side down, and top each oyster with 1 tsp of butter and a bit of the lemon juice.
- Cook for 1 minute; sprinkle the Parmesan cheese over each oyster, then cook for 1 minute more or until the edges of the oyster begin to curl.
- Remove promptly from grill and serve immediately. Pouring additional glasses of champagne is completely appropriate while enjoying the oysters.

Party Drinks

If you've been paying attention to this point, you may have deduced that alcohol has been served in our home. We (usually) try to drink responsibly and we encourage our friends and guests to do so as well; but most people would agree a Chicago Marathon party that runs (no pun intended) from 8am to 6pm would be a bit dreary without the prospect of a Bloody Mary and a pot of coffee.

Back during the days when I was still gainfully employed as a consultant in Cleveland, Marcie threw our first Chicago Marathon party. The next year, I ran the marathon and the party was winding down by the time I arrived back at the condo. I determined then and there that it would be better to pursue my running goals at other races and on other days so I wouldn't miss the party. She does a fantastic job with this party each year and it gives her a chance to show off her cooking prowess. It also allows me a chance to play Sous Chef and bartender.

You'll notice that, for what seemed to me to be obvious reasons, each of these recipes omit the "To Swill while you Grill" selection that appeared in the chapter on appetizers. Don't be discouraged though; these notes will appear once again beginning with breakfast recipes in the next chapter. After all, we have to serve those Bloody Marys and Mimosas sometime!

Bloody Mary Mix

One of my jobs at our Chicago Marathon Party is to prepare our Bloody Mary bar. This is one of my favorite tasks for a morning party as you can be as creative as time, space, and budget allow. My mix recipe is an amalgamation of all of my years in search of the perfect Bloody Mary. This recipe makes a half-gallon pitcher of the mix leaving enough room to avoid a spill when pouring the first glass.

For Chillin' and Swillin'
64 oz Pitcher
Long Handled Spoon
Measuring Spoons
Chef's Knife for cutting garnishes

Ingredients for the Mix
32 oz. tomato juice
16 oz. Clamato juice
5 tbsp. fresh ground horseradish
4 oz. Worcestershire sauce
Juice of 4 limes
Juice of 2 lemons
2 tbsp. celery salt
1 tbsp. lemon pepper
6 tbsp. Tabasco sauce
* 3 tbsp. Salsa Valentina
* 2 tbsp. Maggi
1 tbsp. chili powder

Salt to taste
Back pepper to taste

* Available in the Mexican food section at most grocery stores

Ingredients for the Garnish
4 limes cut into wedges
Celery sticks
Pimento stuffed olives
Dill pickles, halved

Preparation
- Combine and thoroughly stir all of the mix ingredients in a pitcher.
- Serve over ice (with or without Vodka).
- Garnish with the celery, olives, pickles and lime wedges.

Bill Allen

Bloody Mary Bar

For a large gathering like our marathon party, if we haven't hired a bartender, it makes sense to set up the Bloody Mary bar and allow guests to make their own drinks. Assuming your guests are responsible with their alcohol intake, this can save you a lot of work, allow you to interact more with your guests and spend less time making drinks. Only you know your crowd well enough to make that decision.

As I mentioned earlier, your Bloody Mary bar can be as simple or as extravagant as you like. If you've set out your alcohol, filled a bucket with ice, and have iced your mix; the only remaining task is setting out what you would like to have for garnishes. I like to put out some of the mix ingredients so that guests can make their Bloody Marys to their individual tastes, so I'll put out extra limes, horseradish, hot sauce, and salt and pepper along with the pickles, olives, and celery sticks. If I want to step up the garnishes a notch, I'll add skewered grilled shrimp (a variation of my Tequila Lime Shrimp without the tequila) or grilled vegetable skewers containing zucchini, onion, and red bell pepper. I encourage you to play with different variations on the "grilled, skewered" idea. When planning your party, be sure to count these as appetizers if you include them as part of your Bloody Mary bar.

Frozen Chocolate Martini

I struggled with whether to include this recipe as a drink or as a dessert. Truth be told, I've served it more as a frozen after dinner drink in lieu of dessert than anything else. They're absolutely delicious and go down way too easily. I try to limit myself to one or two so that I don't hate myself the next morning. Three could cause you to lapse into a diabetic coma. If you prefer your chocolate martini unfrozen, shake the ingredients over ice, then strain into the martini glasses instead of blending.

For Chillin' and Swillin'
Martini Glasses
Blender

Ingredients
3 oz. vodka
3 oz. Baileys Irish Crème
3 oz. Godiva White Chocolate Liqueur
2 oz. Kahlúa
Powdered chocolate or cocoa
Chocolate syrup
Ice (about 2 cups)
Mint leaves for garnish

Preparation
- Rim the martini glasses with Powdered Chocolate and swirl chocolate syrup into glasses.
- Add ice, vodka, Baileys, Godiva, and Kahlúa to a blender.
- Blend for about 20 seconds or until mixture is frozen but frothy.
- Pour into martini glasses, garnish with a sprig of mint and serve.

Note: You can omit the chocolate syrup and garnish with grated semi-sweet chocolate if you prefer.

Fizzy Redneck Cosmopolitan Martini

Wouldn't you know it? You're having a cocktail party and offer someone a drink. They ask for a Cosmo, and then you suddenly realize that you're out of both Cointreau *and* Triple Sec. What's a genteel host to do? Don't fret. As long as you have a can of lemon lime soda (Sprite, 7-Up, etc.) you may be able to bluff your way through by conjuring up your best Andy Griffith voice (think "Aunt Bea" if you're female) and asking, "How'd ya like to try my famous Fizzy Redneck Cosmopolitan Martini?"

I've done this in an emergency and it worked! It's also a hit with the crowd that likes to mix Bourbon and Mountain Dew while barbequing over a 55 gallon drum.

For Chillin' and Swillin'
Cocktail Shaker
Martini Glasses

Ingredients
1 oz. vodka
2 oz. lemon lime soda
Splash of cranberry juice
Twist of lemon

Preparation
- Combine Vodka, lemon lime soda, and cranberry over ice in a shaker.
- Shake like Mt. St. Helens on May 18th, 1980.
- Strain into a martini glass and garnish with a twist of lime.

The Green Drink (Alejandro's Sister)

I lived the first forty-one years of my life in blissful ignorance of the Green Drink. The Green Drink is a rum-based version of a gin drink called an Alexander's Sister (sans nutmeg) that Marcie's dad, Zeus, serves at his Christmas Day drop-in each year. A friend and neighbor of Zeus started this Christmas Day tradition many years ago in Wisconsin, and Zeus has carried it forward to the present.

There are two kinds of people in this world – those who like the green drink and those who do not. As a math experiment, let's take the number of people who like the green drink, double it and add fifty percent to it. This should give you a number somewhere in the neighborhood of fifteen. If all of the green drink aficionados in the world attend Zeus' Christmas party, and there are one hundred total guests, this means that there are eighty-five of us who must, against our will, endure a glass of green drink at least once annually. Half of the fun for me is discovering the creative locations within the house where people have covertly stashed their green drinks instead of actually consuming them.

Now that the disclaimer is out of the way, the drink is a fun alternative to eggnog and its mint green color makes it a festive looking drink to serve on Christmas Day. Sprinkle a little nutmeg on the drink if you like – I think it softens the taste a little.

Because this recipe uses rum instead of gin, and we all know that rum is primarily produced in Spanish speaking places, I am now renaming this concoction "Alejandro's Sister."

For Chillin' and Swillin'
1 Measuring Cup (1 cup capacity)
Blender
Rocks Glasses

Ingredients
1 part white rum
1 part green Crème de Menthe
1 part heavy cream
2 cups of Ice
Nutmeg (Optional)

Preparation
- Combine all ingredients.
- Blend for 30 seconds or until everyone at the bar is shouting to be heard.
- Turn blender speed up to highest setting to annoy everyone and blend for 10 more seconds.
- Pour into (short) rocks glasses and serve.

Olive Soup

Here's a news flash – Cleveland, Ohio, gets cold in the wintertime. When the wind blows in off of Lake Erie, it only serves to intensify the effect. Sometimes the only way to warm up is by indulging in a few helpings of olive soup.

Billy D., Judy, Ken Steve, and I were regulars on the Cleveland olive soup circuit, and while Judy tended to reunite with "The Captain" during these gatherings and Ken is a confirmed iced tea man nowadays, the rest of us usually opted for olive soup. We debated life-changing quandaries during these gatherings. Questions like:
- Are olives fruits or vegetables?
- Does vermouth and vodka represent a double portion of Vitamin V.?
- If adding olive juice to a martini makes it a Dirty Martini, does omitting it mean you have a Clean Martini?
- Do pitted olives taste better than un-pitted olives?
- Are blue cheese olives the greatest thing that ever happened in the history of the world?
- If one has three olives per martini, is a nine-olive night sufficient to replace dinner?
- Does Billy D. really think that his wife believes "olive soup" is really soup?

In the end, we determined that olive soup should have at least a little bit of olive juice (in order to be soup) and three blue cheese stuffed olives. We also figured that Lisa, Billy D.'s wife, was on to him the whole time.

For Chillin' and Swillin'
Cocktail Shaker
Rocks Glasses

Ingredients
2 ½ oz. vodka (or gin if you prefer)
½ oz. or less vermouth (optional)
½ oz. olive juice
3 blue cheese stuffed olives
Ice

Preparation
- Combine vodka, vermouth, and olive juice over ice in a cocktail shaker.
- Depending on the bartender, we like ours shaken, so give it a good shake - 20 seconds or so should do.
- Strain into a martini glass and garnish with 3 blue cheese olives on a toothpick.

Additional Notes on Parties and Alcohol

Parties are successful or not based on many factors, some you can control, and some you cannot. You can plan your guest list, accounting for how you think your guests will interact with one another. You can plan your menu based on your knowledge of the likes and dislikes of your guests. You can decorate for your party's theme; pair the right wine with each food course, spend a pile of money, and in the end have the party of the year. Or, your party can turn out to be a disaster. As hosts, we tend to think that the smallest thing that goes wrong constitutes a "disaster". Fortunately, most of the things that we perceive as having been less than perfect go unnoticed by everyone except ourselves. (Trust me, no one noticed that the rosemary sprigs on the Prosciutto roll ups were not exactly symmetrical). Most people come to a party to have a good time, enjoy the company of the hosts and the other guests, and to partake of the fantastic food, wine, and festivities that you have gone to so much trouble to arrange. Unfortunately at times, though, there are a few potential turds in the punch bowl that can ruin even the best parties. Let's take a (figurative) look at a few of these and some of the ways to avoid them.

Alcohol

A good bit of the stress of putting together a dinner party and almost all of the stress in putting together a cocktail party revolves around the booze. What wine shall we buy and serve? How much do we need to buy? What if Stacy's pregnant and doesn't know it yet and drinks wine? Will she hate us forever? Does (fill in the name of someone's new girlfriend that you haven't met yet) even drink wine or will she think that her boyfriend hangs around with alcoholic hedonists and, therefore, break up with him causing him to run off and join a monastery in his depression? Okay, which wine and how much to buy are valid questions. I guess that an occasional self-evaluation of one's alcoholic hedonistic tendencies bears checking once in a while as well.

For dinner parties, we'll typically plan on four to five glasses of wine (one bottle) per person. This formula has served us well but it is largely based on our knowledge of the aforementioned alcoholic, hedonistic tendencies of our friends.

Of course, I'm kidding when I make fun of our friends but it brings up a good point. One of the surest ways to have a wrecked party and a potential real disaster is by over-serving your guests and allowing them to drive. It doesn't matter if it's just down the street; don't let your friends drive if they have overindulged. Nothing good can come of it. The last thing you want to do is celebrate your friend's DUI at 4am on a Sunday morning because it's better than hearing that he hurt himself or someone else.

Hiring a bartender for larger parties is also a good idea if it is within your budget to do so. A professional bartender should be trained to know the signs of overindulgence and can often times better keep track of who is drinking how much and how often.

If you are serving alcohol, make sure that there are designated drivers or that you have the number of a taxi company within easy reach. This will allow you to call for a ride for your guest before they have too much time to try to talk you out of it. Better that they be mad at you when they come for their car tomorrow than dead tonight. Better yet, offer to let them spend the night in your guest room. They'll be grateful for a sample of your Bloody Mary recipe in the morning.

The Guest that Never Leaves

All of us have either hosted or heard about parties where it was time to call it a night and there were guests who didn't take the hint that it was time to leave. In these cases, you don't want them to go away mad, you just want them to go away. You don't want to be rude, but you need to do a ten-mile run the next morning and staying awake all night chatting with them is not an option. Here are some ideas:

1. Stifle a yawn and say how beat you are and how great it's been to see them. (Most people will take the hint at this point and leave).
2. Tell them that you wish you could party longer but your doctor has instructed you not to have more than three bottles of wine per night.
3. Tell them that you indiscriminately sleepwalk in the nude and have no recollections of your actions. (It's very important that you only use this option if you think it will make the other person go away).
4. Tell them to "get the hell out" and that "you never want to see them again." This usually works even if they're drunk.

The Food Critic

Unless you're hosting a party as part of a "Top Chef" episode, people will not normally give any unsolicited negative feedback as to your cooking ability. Once in a while, however, someone comes along that has no qualms with sharing his or her expert opinion on your effort. You know, the person who says, "I can't possibly eat this Kobe beef tenderloin that you've prepared because you didn't fly it in here in first class on Japan Airlines and besides, I'm wearing orange and I only eat *Argentine* beef when I'm wearing orange. I eat *Kobe* beef when I'm wearing blue. How could you possibly have not *known* that?"

Short of killing them with your paring knife, you may want to do what I do. Turn a deaf ear on them and don't invite them back for a while. A little ostracizing can go a long way toward fixing this. If you find that it happens again with the same person, the paring knife is going to become an even more attractive option. Don't do it! Just don't invite them back – ordering into a clown's mouth at a drive-thru is probably is better dinner option for someone of their advanced social skills anyway.

A Little Something for the Morning After (Breakfast)

It would be morally wrong for me to write a cookbook that gives you my ideas on how to eat, drink, and become a Bloody Mary, and not at least give you a few breakfast recipes to help you get through the next morning. Besides all of that, breakfast is one of my four or five favorite meals of the day, but because it's usually the first one of the day it's extra-special. Be it traditional, fancy, European, or Mexican, the first meal of the day signifies a new beginning. You've awakened once again (perhaps too soon if you encountered the "guest that never leaves" at your party the night before) and the day has arrived with all of its blessings and challenges. Pour yourself a glass of leftover Bloody Mary mix, maybe even without the alcohol, and get busy enjoying some of these favorites.

Huevos al Bilito (Little Bill's Breakfast Tacos)

The bank that I worked at in Mexico City had a cafeteria that was open for breakfast and lunch each day. After learning just enough Spanish to be dangerous, and getting to know the cafeteria folks at the bank, I was able to communicate to them that I would like to have scrambled eggs mixed with ham, onions, and jalapenos, topped with cheese and served with 3 soft corn tortillas and Pico de Gallo on the side. After ordering this for several days in a row, and to decrease the amount of time that it took to order breakfast each morning, we simply began calling this *Huevos al Bilito con tortillas de maiz*, which loosely translates to Little Bill's Breakfast Tacos. Other people heard me ordering this and started trying it as well. At one point the dish became so popular that it was added as one of the weekly breakfast specials that the cafeteria offered on a rotating basis. Just my little way of advancing international diplomacy and good will.

A couple of points on this recipe. I like to cook it in olive oil but feel free substitute a pat of butter or margarine if you prefer. No, Chihuahua cheese is not made from the milk of a little dog, and yes, you can find it in most Latino markets. Substitute other shredded cheese to vary the flavor. Serve with Jalapeño hash browns and sliced fruit.

For Turnin' and Burnin'
Large Saucepan
Chef's Knife
Cutting Board
Measuring Cup
Measuring Spoons
Tall Glasses for Bloody Marys

Ingredients
1 tbsp. olive oil
2 eggs
2 oz. sliced ham, diced
2 tbsp. chopped onion

1 tbsp. jalapeño pepper, finely chopped
1 oz. milk
1 oz. Chihuahua cheese, shredded
Salt and pepper
3 soft warm tortillas (flour or corn)
Pico de Gallo

To Swill while you Grill

If you're making these on the weekend for houseguests, Bloody Marys are a good idea. If you're just making them for yourself, a Bloody Mary is still a good idea.

Preparation

- Over medium heat, sauté the ham, onion, and jalapeños for 2 minutes or until the onions become translucent.
- Add the eggs (beat them ahead of time if you like, I add mine whole, then scramble) and the milk and scramble with the sautéed ingredients until the eggs are soft and fluffy.
- Salt and Pepper to taste and add the cheese.
- When the cheese has melted, serve with the tortillas and Pico on the side. A couple of slices of melon or papaya can help to give the illusion that you're eating healthy.

Shrimpanadas

Marcie and I have the best of both worlds. We live in Chicago during the warm months and south Florida during the cold months. We're able to be near her mom and step-father, Jan and Jim in the summer and near her dad and step-mother, Zeus and Ally, in the winter, (My mom, Sandra, lives in South Carolina and has yet to see the equity in this arrangement.) It's not surprising that our Florida friends don't visit us nearly as often in Chicago as do our Chicago friends when we're in Florida. Most winters, we have enough out of town visitors that we have to maintain a "guest calendar" to keep everything straight in our minds about who is visiting when. We look with great anticipation toward each set of visitors and the fun we know we'll have with them. Some are up for anything, others prefer to hit the beach and relax, and some are in between.

On Saturday mornings, particularly after particularly intense evenings of vodka and club sodas, the ducks on the pond behind the condo begin squawking way too early. There's nothing like the joy of cooking for your friends after three hours of sleep when the whites of your eyes resemble a strawberry daiquiri. A little jolt and some spicy food are just the prescription. Serve the Shrimpanadas with breakfast potatoes and a mix of cubed melon, papaya, and grapefruit slices. Just make sure that the coffee is on and the Bloody Mary mix is ready by the time anyone else wakes up.

Bill Allen

For Turnin' and Burnin'
12" Saucepan
Chef's Knife
Cutting Board
Cookie Sheet
Rubber Spatula
Tall Glasses for Bloody Marys
Coffee Cups

Ingredients
2 tbsp. olive oil
8 eggs
16 medium shrimp, peeled deveined, and cut into ½ inch chunks
1 medium onion, chopped
2 Jalapeño peppers, seeded and finely chopped
8 oz. shredded Mexican cheese blend
8 – 6" soft tortillas (flour or corn)
1 cup Pico de Gallo

To Swill while you Grill
Again, once you've put the coffee on, Bloody Marys pair nicely with the Shrimpanadas.

Preparation
- Preheat oven to 425 degrees.
- On the stovetop, over medium heat in a 12 inch saucepan, sauté the onions, jalepeños, and ½ cup of the Pico de Gallo for 5 minutes or until the onions become soft and translucent.
- Add the shrimp and gently stir the mixture until the shrimp begin turning pink.
- Add the eggs and scramble with the sautéed ingredients until the eggs are soft and fluffy.
- Remove from heat.
- Spoon the egg mixture onto the tortillas, add cheese and fold into burritos, with the edges of the tortillas on bottom and place on a cookie sheet.
- Top each burrito with additional cheese and bake for 5 minutes until the cheese has melted.
- Serve with breakfast potatoes and additional Pico on the side on each plate. If you have leftover Spicy Shrimp Bisque, try serving this reheated over the Shrimpanadas in place of the Pico sometime.

Sweet and Savory Crepes

Here's a surefire way to impress your guests. Put on your beret and make crepes for breakfast. They're much easier to prepare than you may think and are equally delicious served with sweet or savory fillings. There are a couple of tricks to making crepes that you will easily master with just a little bit of practice. The first is to make the crepe as thin as possible and yet not so thin that the weight of the filling causes it to tear. The second is to cook the crepe until it just begins to turn brown on each side so that remains soft and delicate.

For this recipe, you'll notice that I include sugar as an optional ingredient. Only include the sugar when making sweet crepes. Nothing kills the savory flavor of a mushroom, chive, and Gruyere filled crepe like a tablespoon of sugar.

For Turnin' and Burnin'
Electric Griddle or large nonstick Frying Pan
Blender
Measuring Spoons
Measuring Cups
Chef's Knife
Cutting Board
Rubber Spatula
Champagne Flute

Ingredients (for the crepes)
1 cup all-purpose flour
2 eggs
½ cup milk
½ cup water
1 tbsp. sugar (optional)
2 tbsp. butter
1 tbsp. canola oil
Salt and black pepper (optional)

Ingredients (for the Sweet Filling)
For each crepe, use 2 tablespoons of your favorite sweet filling. Melted semisweet chocolate, pureed fruit, or even fruit preserves straight from the jar will do nicely.

Ingredients (for the Savory Mushroom Chive and Gruyere Filling)
¼ cup mushroom pieces, minced
2 tbsp. chives, chopped
¼ cup, Gruyere cheese, shredded

To Swill while you Grill
I'm already wearing the beret. I'm making crepes. I'm the size of the Louvre. Might as well have some Champagne and complete the picture.

Preparation

- Preheat griddle to 325 degrees and apply a little oil to the griddle with a paper towel.
- In a blender, combine the eggs, flour, butter, milk, and water (sugar too if making sweet crepes) and blend until smooth and creamy.
- Pour 1 cup of the crepe mixture into a measuring cup. From the measuring cup, carefully pour ¼ cup of the mixture onto the griddle for each crepe.
- Cook the crepe for about 1½ minutes or until it begins to brown on the bottom. For savory crepes, feel free to sprinkle a dash of salt and/or black pepper to the crepe once you have poured the batter onto the griddle.
- Turn the crepe and spread 2 tbsp of either the sweet or savory filling over the surface of the crepe.
- Fold the crepe with a spatula beginning at one end and making folds every 2 inches.
- Repeat for each crepe.
- Serve hot.

One-Dish Breakfast Bake

Okay, from the last couple of recipes, you have probably deduced that I am not a stickler for having my eggs separate from my breakfast meat, separate from my potatoes and fruit, etc. This breakfast casserole goes a step further, combining everything (except for, perhaps, toast or coffee) into a single dish. This version of the recipe calls for Chicken Andouille sausage, but I've also made it with traditional breakfast sausage, Italian sausage, and cubed pieces of ham.

For Turnin' and Burnin'
12" Saucepan
Large Mixing Bowl
9" x 13" x 2" Baking Dish
Cutting Board
Measuring Spoons
Chef's Knife
Champagne Flutes

Ingredients
6 eggs
1 lb. chicken Andouille sausage, sliced into ½ inch discs, then halved
2 potatoes, peeled, washed and cut into ½ inch cubes
1 onion, halved and sliced cross wise
2 tbsp. fresh rosemary, minced
1 ½ cups shredded cheddar cheese
2 tsp. salt
2 tsp. black pepper

To Swill while you Grill
I recommend a Mimosa while this dish bakes. Orange juice is good for you.

Preparation
- Preheat oven to 400 degrees.
- Over medium high heat on the stovetop, brown the sausage in a 12" saucepan.
- Once browned, transfer the sausage to a large mixing bowl.
- Beat the eggs and add to the sausage.
- Add the potatoes, onions, rosemary, salt, pepper, and one cup of the cheese.
- Stir until mixed thoroughly.
- Transfer to a 9" x 13" x 2" deep baking dish and cook for 1 hour or until potatoes are cooked throughout.
- Remove from oven and top with remaining ½ cup of cheese.
- Return to oven and cook for 6 – 8 minutes more or until cheese on top is melted and bubbling.

Perfectly Poached Eggs without Gadgets

For the longest time, we bought one gadget after another that promised to make poaching eggs easy and perfect every time. In the end, I went back to the tried and true way. Hot water, eggs, a saucepot, and a slotted spoon make better poached eggs than any of the gadgets out there. It just takes a little practice.

Serve these over toasted bread or an English muffin with fruit for a quick and healthy breakfast.

For Turnin' and Burnin'
2-quart Stockpot
Large Slotted Spoon
Measuring Spoons
Kitchen Towel
Paper Towels
Toaster
Champagne Flutes

Ingredients
1 tsp. olive oil
2 eggs
Toast or English muffins

To Swill while you Grill
I usually hold off until I've finished cooking this dish before having my champagne or Mimosa. I try to make up for it by having 2 glasses during breakfast.

Preparation
- Bring 3 cups of water to a boil.
- Reduce the heat to medium-low.
- When the temperature is holding steady, between 160 and 180 degrees, gently crack the eggs into the water.
- Cook for three minutes.
- While the eggs are poaching, toast the bread or English muffins.
- Retrieve the eggs one at a time from the water with a slotted spoon and set the spoon on a clean kitchen towel to dry.
- Gently pat the top of the egg dry with a second paper towel and serve on the toast or English muffin.
- Repeat for each egg.

Benedict Allen

This recipe is an amalgamation of three other recipes, one of which is an emulsification. (I always told myself that I would use the word "amalgamation" if I ever wrote a book. Emulsification happened just by chance). Place a poached egg over Swiss cheese on a Shrimp 'n Crab Cake. Top with Hollandaise sauce and pair with a Mimosa.

For Turnin' and Burnin'
2-quart Stockpot
Measuring Spoons
Large Slotted Spoon
Kitchen Towel
Paper Towels
Toaster
Champagne Flutes

Ingredients
1 Shrimp 'n Crab Cake
1 slice Swiss cheese
1 poached egg
2 tbsp. Hollandaise sauce

To Swill while you Grill
Same deal as with regular poached eggs. I'll wait until cooking is complete before having my champagne.

Preparation
- Prepare Shrimp 'n Crab Cake according to recipe.
- Prepare egg according to recipe.
- Prepare hollandaise sauce according to recipe.
- Assemble the Benedict by placing the cheese on the seafood cake, the egg on top of the cheese and hollandaise sauce over the egg.
- Serve immediately.

Italian Breakfast Potatoes

This hearty dish can stand on it's own as a breakfast casserole or on the side with a simple cheese and chive omelet. Keeping the potatoes small will reduce the time required in the oven.

For Turnin' and Burnin'

Large Saucepan
Rubber Spatula
Chef's Knife
Cutting Board
Measuring Cup
Measuring Spoons
9" x "13" x 2" Baking dish
Fork
Coffee Cup

Ingredients

3 tbsp. olive oil
2 large potatoes, peeled and cut into 1.2 inch cubes
1 large onion, halved and sliced thinly
6 Italian sausages sliced into ¼ inch discs (mild or hot, depending on your preference)
3 tsp. fresh minced rosemary
2 cloves garlic, minced
1 tsp. salt
1 tsp. Black pepper
6 oz. shredded mozzarella or Asiago cheese.

To Swill while you Grill

Bailey's Irish Cream and Coffee. If you must have cream in your coffee, this is the way to go.

Preparation

- Preheat oven to 425 degrees.
- Sautee the onions, sausage and garlic until the sausages are browned.
- Add sausage mixture, potatoes, rosemary, salt, pepper, and half of the cheese to a 9" x 13" x" 2 inch deep baking dish.
- Sprinkle the remaining cheese on top.
- Cook for 45 minutes or until the potatoes can be easily pierced throughout with a fork.
- Serve hot.

Crispy Jalapeño-Hash Brown Frittatas

The Frittata is perhaps most easily defined as an omelet that is flipped instead of folded. This dish qualifies as a frittata because of the egg used in the recipe but is relegated to the role of supporting actor in this scene. The recipe below yields two side dish portions or 1 breakfast entrée portion. Red jalapeños, along with cilantro make this a colorful as well as spicy dish that will add a little zip to your breakfast.

For Turnin' and Burnin'
Mixing Bowl
Small Saucepan
Grater (for potatoes)
Rubber Spatula
Chef's Knife
Cutting Board
Measuring Cup
Measuring Spoons
9" x "13" x 2" Baking Dish
Fork
Tall glass

Ingredients
3 tbsp. olive oil
1 egg, beaten
1 cup shredded potatoes
1 red jalapeño pepper, seeded and diced
3 tsp. fresh cilantro, diced

To Swill while you Grill
Enjoy a Bloody Maria while preparing the frittata. Just substitute tequila for vodka and make like you would a Bloody Mary.

Preparation
* Combine the egg, potatoes, jalapeño, and cilantro in a bowl and mix well.
* Over medium high heat, in a small saucepan, heat the olive oil until hot.
* Add the potato and egg mixture and spread evenly around the pan.
* Shake the pan periodically to ensure that the frittata does not stick to the pan.
* After 3 to 4 minutes, flip the frittata over. (If "flipping eggs" is not your thing, carefully slide the frittata to a plate, place a second plate on top, and turn the plates over. Return the frittata to the pan.)
* Cook for an additional 3 to 4 minutes or until potatoes are cooked throughout.
* Serve hot.

Rosemary Breakfast Potatoes Au Gratin

After the Bloody Mary, the potato may just be the most vital weapon in your "morning after" arsenal. Many a puny feeling tummy has been made to feel better with the help of our friend, the potato. This is thanks to the alkaline found in potatoes. Simply put, Mr. Potato's alkaline helps to neutralize Mr. Tummy's acid.

I developed this Rosemary Breakfast Potatoes Au Gratin recipe on a particularly bleary-eyed and ill-tempered "morning after". Surprisingly, the onions didn't adversely impact the intended soothing effect of this dish. The rosemary and cheese elevated this breakfast side from the ordinary and by the end of breakfast; I could almost stand to be around myself.

For Turnin' and Burnin'
Large Saucepan
Grater (for potatoes and cheese)
Rubber Spatula
Chef's Knife
Cutting Board
Measuring Cup
Measuring Spoons
9" x "13" x 2" Baking Dish
Rocks Glass

Ingredients
¼ cup olive oil
4 potatoes, peeled and cut into ½ inch cubes
1 onion, halved and sliced cross wise
2 tbsp. fresh rosemary, minced
1 cup shredded cheddar cheese
2 tsp. salt
2 tsp. black pepper

To Swill while you Grill
A crisp Vodka Greyhound will put you in the mood for this potato dish. Think one part vodka, two parts grapefruit juice over ice and stirred.

Preparation
- In a large saucepan over medium-high heat, heat the olive oil.
- Add the potatoes and cook for 10 minutes, stirring often, until they begin to brown.
- Add the onions and cook for 10 more minutes, stirring often.
- After adding the onions, preheat oven to 400 degrees.
- Stir in the rosemary, salt, and pepper and cook for 5 minutes more.
- Remove from heat.
- Transfer to an oiled 9" x 13" x 2" deep baking dish.
- Mix in half of the cheese and top with the remaining cheese.
- Bake for 10 minutes or until cheese on top is bubbling.
- Serve immediately.

Salmon-Rye Breakfast Toast Strips

This is my deconstruction of the lox and bagels classic. A little more "fish forward, if you will. Serve as a side dish with eggs or on its own with all of the normal salmon and bagel accoutrements – red onion, tomatoes, capers, and cream cheese.

For Turnin' and Burnin'
Chef's Knife
Measuring Spoons
Cutting Board
Cookie Sheet
Hurricane Glass

Ingredients
4 slices rye bread
16 slices smoked salmon, sliced very thin
3 tbsp. olive oil
Tomatoes, sliced (for garnish)
Red onion, shaved or chopped (for garnish)
Capers, drained (for garnish)
Cream cheese (for garnish)

To Swill while you Grill
I'm tempted to recommend pairing rye whiskey with the rye bread of the toast but will not. Have a Bloody Mary while you prepare and enjoy this breakfast.

Preparation
- Preheat oven to 425 degrees.
- Cut each piece of rye bread into 4 thin slices and place on cookie sheet.
- Brush Olive oil on both sides of the bread.
- Bake for 8 minutes.
- Remove from oven and carefully wrap a slice of salmon around each toast.
- Return toast to oven and bake for 4 additional minutes.
- Serve immediately.

Soups

Here in America, I think that soup gets a bad rap. Mostly, it's relegated to a choice (as in, "Would you like soup *or* salad with your meal?") or something that you eat when it's really cold outside (no fun there) or when you're sick (even less fun).

"Bring on the meat and potatoes" was always my mantra. Soup, as I saw it, would only take up space that I could otherwise be filling with appetizers and entrees. Although we had soup occasionally while I was growing up, soup for soup's sake was just not something that excited me. Maybe it was because of the enormous cans of soup that I saw in the pantries of the first restaurants in which I worked. Maybe it was because of how that same canned soup looked, smelled, and tasted. Whatever the reason, soup was not my thing. I didn't like to eat it so, therefore, I didn't cook it.

It wasn't until I lived overseas that I developed an appreciation for soups. In both Slovakia and Mexico I discovered that soups didn't have to be the bland, watery, "last-day-before-grocery-shopping" meal that I remembered them as. Soups could add character to a meal on their own, sometimes even being the highlight. This realization pushed me to begin making soups that weren't inspired by the urge to use my can opener.

Spicy Shrimp Bisque

In developing this bisque, I was reminded of the wrath of a single Habanero (Scotch Bonnet) pepper. You'll want to take special care to thoroughly and frequently wash your hands when handling these little guys. Your eyes, nose, and any other sensitive areas will not react well with the capsaicin in the pepper. When taste-testing the bisque, if you find it to be too spicy, adding milk will help to diffuse the heat. I like to serve this dish in a champagne flute, each flute topped with one sautéed Tequila Lime Shrimp as a garnish. For my own amusement, depending on the crowd, I will also serve the bisque with a soupspoon to see who uses the spoon and who drinks it directly from the flute (I'm okay with either).

For Turnin' and Burnin'
2-quart Stockpot
Measuring Cup (2-cup size is ideal, but 1 cup size will do)
Measuring Spoons
Chef's Knife
Cutting Board
Colander
Food Processor or Blender
Long Handled Cooking Spoon
Tasting Spoon
Champagne Flutes (this time actually for the food!)
Shot Glass (sorry, it's for the side serving of milk!)
Bottle Opener (at last, something for the chef)

Bill Allen

Ingredients
2 tbsp. olive oil
8 medium shrimp, peeled, deveined, and chopped
1 Habanero pepper, seeded and chopped
2 medium potatoes, peeled and cut into 1 inch cubes
2 carrots, peeled and cut into 1 inch pieces
1 onion, chopped
2 tomatoes, seeded and chopped
2 cloves garlic, chopped
Kosher salt to taste
Black pepper to taste
1 quart of Milk
Diced cilantro for garnish

To Swill while you Grill
My advice to you, Dear Chef, is that you have a couple of beers ready while you cook the bisque. At some point during the tasting process, you will want something readily at your disposal to pour on top of the burning that suddenly overwhelms your mouth.

Preparation
- In 2 cups of boiling water, add the olive oil, shrimp, potatoes, carrots, onions, tomatoes, garlic, and half of the Habanero pepper.
- Cook for 15 minutes or until the potatoes become tender.
- Strain through a colander, reserving 1 cup of the liquid.
- Puree the shrimp and vegetable mixture in a food processor or blender.
- Add ¼ cup of the reserved liquid to the pot and reduce heat to medium-low.
- Add the puree back to the pot.
- Stir in ½ cup of the milk.
- Salt and Pepper to taste.
- Cook for 30 minutes more, stirring frequently.
- Add salt, pepper and milk as necessary to adjust for spiciness.
- Serve in champagne flutes and garnish with a sautéed Tequila Lime Shrimp over the rim and a sprinkle of diced cilantro on top of the bisque.
- A shot glass of milk served along side makes an interesting accompaniment as well.

Chicken Soup for the Belly

This is the one to cook when it's cold outside, or someone you love has a cold on the inside. Additionally, it is the base chicken soup recipe that will be referenced for the Avgolemono and Chicken Tortilla soups that follow.

For Turnin' and Burnin'

6-quart Stockpot
Measuring Cup (2-cup size is ideal, but 1 cup size will do)
Measuring Spoons
Long Handled Cooking Spoon
Tasting Spoon
Chef's Knife
Cutting board
2 Forks
Wine Glass
Corkscrew

Ingredients

2 tbsp. olive oil
1 small chicken, skin left on and cut into pieces
2 carrots, peeled and cut into 1 inch pieces
1 onion, chopped
2 celery stalks, cut into ¼ inch pieces
Kosher salt
Black pepper
1 sprig of fresh rosemary, minced
1 tbsp. fresh thyme
8 oz. package white or yellow rice

To Swill while you Grill

I'm going to assume here that you're not the one who is sick. If you are, someone else should be making chicken soup for you! That said, Pinot Noir is a choice red that will pair nicely with the aroma of the simmering soup.

Preparation

- Stew the chicken pieces, olive oil, and a tablespoon of salt in a large stockpot in approximately 3 quarts of water, or enough to easily cover the chicken for about 45 minutes or until the chicken is cooked through.
- Remove the chicken from the water and set aside on a cutting board.
- Add the carrots, onion, celery, rosemary, and time to the broth along with a teaspoon of salt and black pepper.
- Once the chicken has cooled (enough to where you won't need to go to the emergency room if you touch it), remove and discard the skin.
- Separate the meat from the bones, discarding the bones.
- Shred (using 2 forks) or chop the chicken meat into small pieces and return it to the stockpot with the rice.
- Bring to a boil and stir for 1 minute.
- Reduce heat to simmer, salt and pepper to taste and let cook for 1 hour.
- Adjust seasoning to taste and serve with crackers.

"Which Came First" the Avgo or the Lemono?

Upon returning north from our first winter in Florida, the weather was not kind to my betrothed. We arrived in Chicago just in time for an April cold snap that left Marcie sick and in bed for Easter weekend. Since it seemed that she was not up to having lamb for Easter, I made her Kotosopa Avgolemono (Egg-Lemon Chicken Soup), substituting white rice for yellow rice and using the additional ingredients and preparation steps below.

For Turnin' and Burnin' (in addition to previous chicken soup recipe)
None

Ingredients (in addition to previous chicken soup recipe)
2 eggs
Juice of 1 lemon
8 oz. white rice to replace yellow rice (optional)

To Swill while you Grill
If you can find a Greek, Cypriot, or Croatian white wine, this is the time to drink it. In the absence of any of these, go with a Pinot Blanc.

Preparation
*   Prepare Chicken Soup for the Belly. Use white rice in place of yellow rice if desired.
*   Once complete, beat 2 eggs in a large mixing bowl and add the lemon juice.
*   Gradually add 2 cups of the chicken soup stock to the egg-lemon mixture, stirring constantly so that the eggs don't curdle.
*   Return the egg-lemon-broth mixture to the soup, still stirring continually.
*   Serve immediately.

Chicken Tortilla Soup

The first time that I ever ate chicken tortilla soup (or Vera Cruz style red snapper for that matter) in Mexico was at a fancy restaurant called La Antigua Hacienda de Tlalpan. (Come to think of it, it's also the only place where I've eaten ant eggs.) This former home had been renovated into a restaurant with an enormous dining room, bar, and one of the largest outdoor dining patios that I have ever seen. The grounds were complete with both regular and Albino peacocks and peahens. Given the beauty of the setting, it's no wonder that many weddings, both real and the televised soap opera variety take place there.

I substitute small potato cubes for the rice and add jalapeños or serranos to the base chicken soup recipe described earlier along with the carrots, onions, and celery. Substitute cilantro for rosemary as well and sprinkle additional chopped cilantro right before serving. Thin strips of tortilla chips, lime wedges, and small slices of avocado complete the dish.

For Turnin' and Burnin' (in addition to previous chicken soup recipe)
Margarita Glass (if you plan to have a margarita)
Bottle Opener (if you plan to have a beer)

**Ingredients** **(in addition to previous chicken soup recipe)**
2 potatoes, peeled and cut into ½ inch cubes
2 tbsp. fresh cilantro, plus cilantro for garnish
4 jalepeños, seeded, washed, and cut into thin strips
Lime wedges
Thin, fried tortilla strips
1 avocado, peeled, seeded and cut into small slices

**To Swill while you Grill**
Margaritas or beers. Period.

**Preparation**
- Prepare Chicken Soup for the Belly.
- Add the potatoes at the same time as the onions and carrots
- When soup is ready to be served, add additional chopped cilantro to each bowl.
- Serve with side dishes of cilantro, avocado slices, tortilla strips, and lime wedges. Additional diced jalepeños may be served on the side as well.

New England Seafood Chowder

On a cool evening, we sometimes like to do heartier soups instead of an entrée. Given all of the fresh seafood that we have access to in Florida, seafood chowder is an easy choice. Marcie is a fan of New England style chowders, so I make this one for her whenever the South Florida winter temperature plummets below 70 degrees. While I cook, she'll bundle up in a sweater and pretend that we're in Chicago or Wisconsin or some other cold place. To make this as a traditional clam chowder, add an additional 6 ounces of clams and omit the other seafood.

**For Turnin' and Burnin'**
12" Saucepan, 3" deep
Measuring Cup
Measuring Spoons
Long Handled Cooking Spoon
Potato Peeler
Tasting Spoon
Chef's Knife
Cutting Board
Wine Glass
Corkscrew

Bill Allen

Ingredients
2 tbsp. olive oil
2 strips of bacon, chopped into ¼ inch squares
1 onion, chopped
1 carrot, peeled diced into ¼ inch pieces
1 celery stalk, diced into ¼ inch pieces
32 oz. chicken broth
1 large potato, peeled, washed and cut into ½ inch cubes
¼ cup dry white wine
6 oz. Half and Half
1 tsp. fresh rosemary, minced
2 tsp. fresh thyme
12 oz. chopped clams (steamed or canned)
6 oz. lump crab meat
6 oz. medium shrimp, peeled and deveined

To Swill while you Grill
Sauvignon Blanc is a favorite of mine while preparing white chowders.

Preparation
- Over medium high heat, sauté the olive oil, bacon, and onions for 3 minutes.
- Add the carrots and celery and cook for 1 minute more.
- Add the chicken broth and bring to a boil.
- Add the potatoes and white wine, cover, and cook for 10 minutes.
- Turn heat down to simmer.
- Add the Half and Half, rosemary, thyme, salt and pepper to taste, stir and cook uncovered for 5 minutes.
- Add the seafood and cook uncovered for 5 minutes more or until shrimp are pink and cooked through.
- Continue simmering and stirring until chowder thickens a bit, for 2 or 3 minutes more.
- Serve with oyster crackers or crusty bread and a glass of Sauvignon Blanc.

Slovak Kapustnica (Cabbage and Sausage Soup)

By the fall of 1992, I had never ventured further west than Alabama, much less traveled outside of the United States. All of that changed when I accepted a traveling gig as a consultant with a firm that sold software and consulting services to banks around the world. During the hiring process, we had the typical conversation that one would have with their new employer before accepting a position that required travel.

There were the typical questions that the resource management person asked while interviewing me over the telephone.

"How do you feel about traveling?" she asked.

"I'm looking forward to it," was my response.

"We do business with about 150 clients in twenty countries," she said enthusiastically.

"That's great!" I responded. "Like, where?"

"Australia, Europe, all over Asia. And of course, the U.S."

"I understand that my initial assignment would be in Phoenix," I said.

"Yes, but we'd like to get an idea if you would be willing to travel internationally as well," she replied.

"Absolutely!," I said quickly. Then thinking for a second I asked, "I wouldn't have to go to Iran or something, would I?"

"No," she laughed. "We don't have any clients over there just yet."

So I took the job, and after a whirlwind eight months of traveling cross-country from Charlotte to Phoenix every week, I was approached about the possibility of taking an assignment in Europe. Immediately, I thought about Buckingham Palace, The Eifel Tower, the Spanish Riviera, and cuckoo clocks in the Black Forest of Germany. When I learned that the assignment was in Bratislava, Slovakia, the only pictures that came to mind were of borscht, sad people dressed in gray, and border crossings with lots of armed guards. That and fantastic beer. Because of the beer, I took the assignment.

If you've never been to Slovakia (and even if you have), I'm thrilled to report that I have seldom been as utterly wrong in prejudging a place as I was with Bratislava. Don't get me wrong, the beer was as good as advertised, but I was wrong about just about everything else.

Borscht (a classic Russian Beet Soup) is not commonly served in Slovakia. Almost all of the people that I met during my almost two years in country were friendly and happy. People wore colors other than gray and border crossings were relatively painless.

One of Slovakia's most abundantly available vegetables is the cabbage. The Slovaks make a wonderful cabbage and sausage (or ham) soup that is a staple of most restaurant menus in Bratislava. My version includes kidney beans for a little extra texture and body and both sausage and ham because I hate to decide between the two.

For Turnin' and Burnin'

12" Saucepan, 3" deep
Measuring Cup
Measuring Spoons
Long Handled Cooking Spoon
Tasting Spoon
Chef's Knife
Cutting Board
Bottle Opener
Pilsner Glass (optional)

Ingredients

1 green cabbage, cored and chopped
2 tbsp. olive oil
12 oz. kielbasa, cut into ¼ inch discs
12 oz. ham, cut into ½ inch cubes
12 oz. canned kidney beans
3 cloves garlic, minced
Salt
Black pepper
Paprika
Sour cream

To Swill while you Grill

Unless you can find a bottle of Frankovka (Slovak red wine), a couple of Pilsner Urquells or Czechvars will do fine to make you think that you've died and gone to Bratislava.

Preparation

- Add the cabbage and kidney beans to 2 quarts of hot water and bring to a boil.
- Boil for 10 minutes, and then reduce heat to simmer.
- While the cabbage is boiling, sauté the kielbasa and the garlic in the little olive oil for two minutes and add to the soup.
- Add the ham and continue to cook uncovered over low heat for 1 hour, adjusting salt, pepper, and paprika to taste.
- Ladle in soup bowls and top with a dollop of sour cream.
- Serve with crusty bread on the side. Pair with a cold bottle of Pilsner Urquell.
- Say "Na zdravie! (To your health!)"

Beef

When my dad was a little boy, I'm guessing about four or five years old, my grandmother asked him what he would like to have for lunch. In what should have become one of the famous recipe names of all time, my dad replied, "I'd like an all meat sandwich please!"

Beef represents everything I love about eating. It's grill friendly, happy to be cooked rare, extra well (think shoe leather), or any temperature in between. It's the ultimate "man comfort food". (Okay, lasagna is "man comfort food" too, but that's for another chapter). Be it a burger, a steak, cooked in a wok or tagine, wrapped in a Slovak potato pancake, or adding flavor, texture, and body to an Italian red sauce, beef is the conduit for an extraordinary number dishes all over the world.

Argentine Style Grilled Whole Beef Tenderloin

I had the opportunity to work on a software engagement in Argentina for a couple of years in the mid-1990's. Buenos Aires is a fascinating city, vibrant and full of European as well as Latin American culture. Argentina is world-renowned for its grass fed beef. Properly prepared Argentine beef tenderloin can almost be cut using a fork.

A staple of Argentine culture is the Asado. Literally translated, asado means "to roast," but in this case it's a noun - their version of a cookout.

Given that many Argentines trace their roots to Europe in general and Italy specifically, spicy chili peppers are not a staple of Argentine cooking. Garlic on the other hand is. Think of this recipe as if your typical non-Italian looking Italian (me) got hold of a beautiful whole tenderloin of beef, decided to cook it on a grill and said, "how do I want this to taste?" That's how Argentine Bife de Lomo is done at an asado. I like to top this with a peppercorn and red wine reduction (either Malbec or Zinfandel) and serve with either garlic mashed potatoes or peeled grilled roasted potatoes. Pair with a glass of Malbec or Tempranillo.

For Turnin' and Burnin'
Outdoor Grill
Large Mixing Bowl
Measuring Cup
Measuring Spoons
Long Handled Spoon
Chef's Knife
Cutting Board
Grill Tongs
Instant Read Meat Thermometer
Bottle Opener
Corkscrew
Bottle Opener
Wineglass

Bill Allen

Ingredients

6 cloves fresh garlic, minced
4 tbsp. olive oil
½ cup onion, finely chopped
2 tbsp. kosher salt
1 tbsp. black pepper
4 tbsp. rosemary, minced
1 whole beef tenderloin, cleaned of excess fat and all silver skin
1 glass of Malbec, Tempranillo, or other red wine
1 Quilmes beer or other light flavored lager

To Swill while you Grill

To get the Argentine asado vibe going, Malbec and Tempranillo are two favorites. Of course, since I'm a little less sophisticated, a beer also pairs nicely with the aroma of meat grilling over an open flame.

Preparation

- Mix first 6 ingredients together in a bowl and transfer to a one gallon freezer storage bag.
- Add the whole tenderloin to the bag, close the bag and shake until the marinade thoroughly covers the beef.
- Refrigerate for at least 30 minutes but no more than 1 hour.
- Take a sophisticated friend, the glass of wine, and the beer with you as you go outside to the grill. Hand your friend the glass of wine and tell them if they were less sophisticated, they could have had a beer as well.
- Carefully place the tenderloin on the grill, making sure to pour the remaining marinade over the beef.
- Toast your friend's health by saying "Salud!" and watch the beef cook for about 20 minutes.
- Turn the beef using tongs and cook for another 20 minutes or so or until the center of the beef is 130 degrees for rare or 140 degrees for medium rare.
- Remove tenderloin from grill and tent with foil on a carving board for 15 minutes.
- Carve into ½ inch slices, arrange on a large platter, and serve.

Standing Rib Roast with New Potatoes

For most of us, having Prime Rib is something that we do in a restaurant, not at home. And with good reason! It's expensive, time consuming to prepare, and your cooking reputation is on the line whenever you serve a rib roast at a party. You'll either be a hero or zero in twenty (or so) not so easy steps. Make a flavorful crust and cook the rib to just the right temperature and your guests will treat you like a rock star and commit to buy 100 copies of your cookbook. Make a dry, overcooked roast and your cookbook will become preferred kindling for the Wisconsin winter. From Wisconsin to Florida and everywhere in between, this is a dish for special occasions like Easter, Christmas, winning the lottery, or cooking for your in-laws. You don't want to screw up Easter dinner (especially if you've invited your in-laws over).

Let's say you're planning to serve Easter Sunday dinner for eight people at 7:30pm. If you have an eight-pound, four bone roast (even better if donated by your mother in-law), you'll have salted the roast on Saturday and refrigerated over night. Marinate your roast with my Prime Rib Marinade at 3pm on Sunday. By 5pm, you'll want to have the roast in the oven. Invite your dinner guests to come over at around 4:30pm. That way, they can watch the back nine of the final round of the Masters while you cook dinner. Put out some apps, show them where the drinks are and leave them alone to watch golf.

Serve the rib with its juices (au jus) and sauces that you like. I like to serve the beef with side dishes of horseradish cream sauce, prepared horseradish from the market, and toasted garlic bleu cheese cream sauce. Drink a big red wine like with this – Petit Sirah is a favorite of mine.

For Turnin' and Burnin'
Large Mixing Bowl
Measuring Cup
Measuring Spoons
Chef's Knife
Grill Tongs
Cutting Board
Kitchen Fork
Instant Read Meat Thermometer
Corkscrew
Wineglass

Ingredients
1 cup Prime Rib Marinade
1 8 lb. (4 bone) standing rib roast, bone in
2 lbs. new potatoes
1 onion, cut into wedges
Salt

To Swill while you Grill
If you're having guests for a special meal, it's a nice touch to decant your red wine. While doing so, privately, make sure a little bit of the Petit Sirah, Syrah, or Cabernet Sauvignon that you will be serving finds it's way into a wine glass for the chef.

Preparation
- 1 day before cooking, rub the roast in 3 tbsp of salt and refrigerate.
- The next day, about two hours before you plan to begin cooking the roast, remove from the refrigerator in order for the beef to come to room temperature. This will allow for a proper "crust-to-center" cooking temperature relationship.
- Coat the roast in the prime rib marinade and let stand in the roasting pan.
- Preheat oven to 450 degrees.
- Add ½ cup water and ½ cup of red wine to the roasting pan.
- Add the potatoes and onion wedges.
- Sprinkle salt and black pepper on potatoes and onions.

- Cook at 450 degrees for 15 minutes. Reduce heat to 325 degrees and cook for 60-75 minutes or until center of roast is 120 degrees (for rare) when checked with an instant read meat thermometer.
- This is your chance to mingle with your guests and bask in their praise of how good dinner smells.
- When the beef reaches an internal temperature of 120 degrees, remove from the oven.
- Unless you're going Flintstones style, carefully remove the rib bones from the roast and let the beef stand for 15 to 20 minutes, loosely covered in foil. The beef will continue to cook internally while standing.
- Transfer the potatoes to a serving bowl and cover with foil.
- If making Yorkshire pudding, reserve 1 cup of the drippings, otherwise discard fat.
- Place the roasting pan and its remaining juices over two burners on medium high heat.
- Add 1 cup of beef stock and ½ cup of red wine to the juices and cook for about 5 minutes.
- Salt and pepper to taste.
- Strain au jus into a gravy boat.
- Carve beef into ½ inch slices, arrange on a large platter, and serve with the au jus and potatoes.

Prosciutto and Gorgonzola Flank Steak Pinwheels

As a child, the first time I saw pinwheels behind the butcher's counter of the grocery store, I thought, "Wow, cool!

I wonder how they made those!" The appearance of this dish belies the fact that it's not very difficult to make. I like to use flank steak for pinwheels because of the way its flavor stands up to the other ingredients; equally important, it's quite resilient to a tenderizing hammer. I've tried a number of different ingredients along with the flank steak and Prosciutto (think spinach, provolone cheese) and you should as well. The prep time will be well worth it when you see and taste the finished product.

For Turnin' and Burnin'
Outdoor Grill
Measuring Spoons
Chef's Knife
Cutting Board
Grill Tongs
Corkscrew
Wineglass

Ingredients

1 ¼ lbs. flank steak, pounded to ¼ inch thickness with a tenderizing hammer

2 tbsp. olive oil

2 garlic cloves, minced

3 oz. Prosciutto de Parma

4 oz. Gorgonzola cheese, softened

1 tsp. kosher salt

½ tsp. ground black pepper

To Swill while you Grill

Pinwheel cooking is the perfect time for a Bourbon Manhattan. They cook quickly enough that you'll only have time enough to enjoy one. That's probably for the best. Once dinner is on the table, pair with a Merlot or other red that won't overpower the flavors of the dish.

Preparation

- Preheat grill to 350 degrees.
- On a cutting board, coat both sides of the flattened beef with the olive oil, garlic, salt, and pepper.
- Evenly place the Prosciutto on top of the beef.
- Evenly spread the cheese on top of the Prosciutto.
- Beginning at the edge of the beef closest to you, carefully roll the beef tightly away from you until it is in the shape of a tube.
- Square the right end of the tube with a carving knife (do this on the left end if you're left handed).
- Beginning ½ inch from the squared end, place skewers through the tube at 1 inch intervals.
- Cut out the pinwheels by slicing the through the tube between each of the skewers.
- Grill for 3 to 4 minutes on each side for medium rare.

Beef Tenderloin Tartare

First, the disclaimer. Eating raw or undercooked meat, eggs, or seafood can be bad for you. Serving it to someone else is even worse. Be sure to take extra care when working with and serving this or any other dish that features raw or undercooked proteins and live by the adage, "When in doubt, throw it out!" (Okay, now that I've made my attorney happy, we can move on to beef tartare).

One of the last things they teach you in steakhouse-meat-cutter-university is how to clean beef tenderloin. It's understandable as the price of tenderloin seemingly rivals that of gold. The importance of cleaning the tenderloin in a manner which produces the least amount of fat and trimmings is of utmost importance to save on cost; therefore, one typically learns to cut on less expensive pieces of meat before moving on to the more expensive cuts.

This background has given me a mindset of frugality when cleaning whole tenderloin for home use and Beef Tartare is an excellent vehicle for utilizing pieces of the tenderloin that are too small to be used for steaks. Whether you buy your tenderloin whole or already cut into steaks is not important. What is important is that if you occasionally enjoy beef on the incredible rare side (cold and completely uncooked), Beef Tartare is a special treat. Make sure to use fresh beef and keep the beef cold before preparing and chill again before serving.

For Turnin' and Burnin'
Large Mixing Bowl
Measuring Cup
Measuring Spoons
Chef's Knife
Cutting Board
Corkscrew
Wineglass

Ingredients
For the Beef Tartare
1 tsp. capers, drained and chopped
1 tsp. Dijon mustard
1 tsp. Worcestershire sauce
1 tsp. onion, minced
1 garlic clove, minced
1 tbsp. olive oil
½ tsp. salt
½ tsp black pepper
1 egg
1 lb. fresh beef tenderloin, finely chopped or ground
½ tsp. ground black pepper

For the Garnishes
16 pieces Melba toast
¼ cup capers, drained
¼ cup red onions, chopped
Dijon mustard

To Swill while you Grill
There's really not much down time to enjoy an adult beverage while doing all of the chopping and mixing but try sipping on a glass of Beaujolais as you have time.

Preparation
- Wash your hands.
- Add the capers to a mixing bowl and mash them thoroughly.
- Mix in the mustard, Worcestershire, onion, garlic, olive oil, salt, pepper, and egg.
- Add the tenderloin and mix it with the other ingredients.
- Wash your hands again.
- Form the beef into a mound and place on a large serving platter.
- Wash your hands a third time.
- Refrigerate for 30 minutes.
- Arrange toast and garnishes around the beef and serve.

Shaved Tenderloin Steak Sandwich Pita

I lived on and off with Nana and Grandpa Bonanno, my mom's parents, from the time I was seventeen years old until I was twenty-two. It was during this time that I fully discovered my grandmother's talent for turning almost any food into a sandwich. Wrap anything in a little bread and butter and you have a sandwich. Green beans? No problem. Vegetable Soup? Just put it on a piece of bread and eat it fast before it becomes soggy. Even though Nana never seemed to gain a pound, she loved bread more than anyone I have ever known.

It was during one of my extended stays with my grandparents that my grandfather helped me to get a job cooking at a diner in Florida City, Florida. This was the every-other-day-thirteen-hours-a-day gig where I cooked breakfast, lunch, and dinner.

We did a grilled steak and onion sandwich there that was the most popular item on the lunch menu. I've adapted the recipe over the years but have stayed true to the basic concept.

This recipe features Nana's favorite use of bread – as a handle for a sandwich. Just to be different, I stuff a grilled pita with the steak, onion, and cheese.

For Turnin' and Burnin'
Large Mixing Bowl
Measuring Cup
Measuring Spoons
Chef's Knife
Butcher's Knife or Slicer (you can also ask your butcher to shave the tenderloin)
Cutting Board
Hurricane Glass

Ingredients
1 medium onion, sliced into thin rings
8 oz. shaved beef tenderloin
3 tbsp. olive oil
4 oz. shredded mozzarella cheese
2 pita pockets

To Swill while you Grill
Sip a Bloody Mary while making this for lunch. While you could certainly serve this as a dinner entrée, I tend to think of this as a brunch or lunch dish. Partly because it's sandwich-like and partly because I don't typically drink Bloody Marys at night.

Preparation

- Preheat an electric skillet grill to 350 degrees.
- In a large bowl, mix the beef with the Italian dressing so that the dressing thoroughly coats the meat.
- Sautee the onions in 2 tbsp. of the olive oil until the onions soften and become translucent, about 4 minutes.
- Add the beef and cook until the beef is thoroughly browned, about 2 more minutes.
- Divide the mixture in half and top with the mozzarella cheese.
- Brush the remaining olive oil on the pitas and grill on each side for about 1 minute.
- Stuff each pita with the steak, onion, and cheese mixture and serve.

Game

The nature of my previous career – the one that I had before becoming a full time dog walker – was such that, whenever I was working in the U.S., I would travel to the same client site each week and home on the weekends for the duration of my assignment. These assignments usually lasted for more than one year, sometimes as much as four or five years. A huge benefit in this type of arrangement is that, if you hate your client, hate the place you are working, or just plain would like a change, you know that the assignment will not last forever. The downside, of course, is that if you love your project, client, or the fabulously exotic place that you are assigned, you know that your assignment will eventually come to an end and you will have to say your goodbyes.

Because the software I have worked with is somewhat specialized, the pool of consultants who work with it is fairly small. This means that when projects end, goodbyes are often times temporary and that you'll see these friends and colleagues on future assignments. That's a double-sided coin as well but, for the most part, I've enjoyed reconnecting with the people that I've worked with in the past.

One of the more interesting people that I've met in my travels is a fellow named Brent. His political views are a little to the right of Attila the Hun. He thinks that deer hunting should be taught in public schools, and has never sung a song at karaoke that was written after his parents were born. Judy (whom you may remember from my recipe for Olive Soup) can attest to this last point. Considering that Brent is in his early forties, his song selection is pretty much limited to the hits of Frank Sinatra and Judy Garland.

You've probably surmised from the title of this section and from my reference to Brent's views on public school curriculum that he is an avid hunter. I am not. As I enjoy fishing, it's not some deep ethical or moral conviction that drove my decision not to hunt. I just don't see the appeal of sitting in a tree stand in the freezing cold, for hours on end, wearing some awful orange vest so that other people don't shoot you instead of the deer…. My motto is, "You kill it and I'll cook it." And that's precisely what Brent did.

"Game Over" Stuffed Venison Tenderloin

The weekend that Marcie and I got married, Brent drove from Cleveland, Ohio to Florida for the wedding. When he stopped by the house, he was carrying a small cooler. Figuring that he had some leftover beers from the ride, I asked him, "Need to put that beer in the fridge?"

"This ain't beer pal, it's deer," he replied.

"I guess it'll need to go in the freezer then," I responded.

He opened the cooler and presented me with a two pound venison tenderloin. It was so beautiful that I almost cried. (Being a non-hunter, I'm completely at the mercy of my friends who hunt to provide me with venison.)

I call this "Game Over" Venison Tenderloin because the wine and vinegar marinade that I use eliminates the gaminess that is normally associated with deer meat.

Bill Allen

For Turnin' and Burnin'
Gene, Gene, the Grillin' Machine
Cutting Board
Butcher Knife
Chef's Knife
Measuring Cup
Measuring Spoons
Toothpicks
Large Bowl
1 Gallon Ziploc Bag
Carving Knife
Corkscrew
Wine Glass

Ingredients
¼ cup olive oil
3 tbsp. fresh rosemary, finely chopped
3 cloves garlic, minced
3 strips turkey bacon, chopped
¼ cup red wine vinegar
½ cup dry red wine
2 lb. venison tenderloin, cleaned
4 red jalapeño peppers, seeded and chopped
½ cup Parmesan cheese, grated
2 tsp. salt
2 tsp. black pepper

To Swill while you Grill
You'll want to have a big red wine that will not be overpowered by the richness of the venison. Either a Super Tuscan or California Syrah will do nicely. Because decisions like this can be difficult, start out with the Syrah while you're grilling, and move to the Super Tuscan during dinner.

Preparation
* In a large bowl, combine the olive oil, rosemary, garlic, vinegar, wine, and half of the salt and pepper. Stir until thoroughly mixed.
* Butterfly the tenderloin lengthwise.
* Place the tenderloin into the Ziploc bag and carefully pour the marinade into the bag.
* Close the bag completely and shake for a few seconds to cover the meat in the marinade.
* Refrigerate for 1 – 2 hours.
* Preheat grill to 375 degrees (medium high heat).
* Remove tenderloin from the refrigerator. Discard marinade.

- Lay the tenderloin cut side up on a cutting board.
- Distribute the turkey bacon, jalapeños, and half of the cheese over the center (cut part) of the loin.
- Fold the loin together to close.
- Add remaining salt and pepper as well as cheese to outside of the loin.
- Secure the loin with toothpicks at 2-inch intervals.
- Grill for 20 minutes or until venison is 145 degrees (for medium rare).
- Remove from oven and let rest for 5 minutes.
- Remove toothpicks, carve into medallions, and serve.

Lamb

Everyone loves Curly. (No, not the guy from the Three Stooges, though I think that he's pretty hysterical too). Curly Lambeau, named after the first coach of the Green Bay Packers, is our ninety-pound, silver standard poodle. As a Miami Dolphins fan, I've already cast my vote for our next dog's name to be Larry Czonka.

When Marcie and I started dating, and she, the Wisconsin girl, told me that she had a poodle, I thought he would be one of those show dogs with frou-frou hair and painted nails and generally a precocious and spoiled pain in the neck or some other part of the anatomy where one hopes to never feel pain. She indicated that if Curly didn't like me that I would be out. Fortunately for yours truly, Curly and I hit if off quite well. I learned that he has quite a fondness for lamb and sweet potato treats. I'm sure that he still thinks he has the upper hand in our relationship.

I was quite surprised to find Curly to be able to balance his prior life as a "Mama's boy" with that of being a "guy's dog". This is despite the efforts of our friends Rod and Pat to replace his manly red bandana with a pink and chartreuse one. He likes to chase (and destroy) tennis balls, carry small tree limbs around in his mouth, and howl like a coyote whenever he's left alone. Typical guy.

There's only one problem. By the time he's due for a trip to the groomer, for a bath and haircut, he looks like a goat. Marcie says he looks like a lamb, but I think it's more the wooly-goat look.

Curly is quite the fan of lamb and brown rice. Unfortunately for him, his comes in kibble form. Luckily for the rest of us, we get to enjoy lamb in a more traditional way.

Herb-Rubbed Boneless Leg of Lamb

When your father in-law's name is Zeus, you'd better have a "go-to" lamb recipe or two in your repertoire. The end result is a delicious entrée that you'll want to make over and over again. This dish calls for artichoke hearts but feel free to substitute potatoes if you like. Wilted Spinach with Bacon as a side dish rounds out the meal.

For Turnin' and Burnin'
Cutting Board
Chef's Knife
Measuring Cup
Measuring Spoons
Kitchen String
Large Bowl
Carving Knife
Corkscrew
9" x 13" Baking Dish
Wine Glass

Ingredients
½ cup olive oil
1 tbsp. fresh mint, finely chopped
1 tbsp. fresh parsley, finely chopped
2 tbsp. fresh rosemary, finely chopped
3 cloves garlic, minced
4-5 lb. boneless leg of lamb
6 oz. cooked artichoke hearts
Salt
Pepper

To Swill while you Grill
If Zeus and Ally are coming over for dinner, we'll decant our nicest bottle of Zinfandel at least an hour before they arrive. While I'm cooking, Marcie and I will share our fourth or fifth nicest bottle of Zin. That way, nicest bottles two and three will still be in reserve if we need them.

Preparation
- Pour olive oil into a measuring cup.
- Combine the mint, parsley, rosemary, and garlic to the oil and mix well.
- Spread the lamb out over a cutting board
- Rub the herb marinade over the both sides of the lamb.
- Sprinkle salt and pepper on the lamb.
- Roll the lamb up and tie with kitchen string in 2 inch intervals.
- Place in a large bowl, cover and Refrigerate for 1 hour.
- Preheat oven to 350 degrees.
- Add ½ cup of water, lamb, and artichokes to baking dish.
- Cook for 45 minutes or until internal temperature reaches 140 degrees on an instant read thermometer for medium rare, 150 degrees for medium.
- Remove from oven and let rest for 5 – 10 minutes.
- Remove kitchen string, carve, and serve.

Goat Cheese-Tapenade Stuffed Lamb Chops

There is no pressure like that of cooking for the girlfriends of your girlfriend. Okay, I'm obviously exaggerating, but only to make a point. There are very few things that can strike fear into the heart of a man in a new relationship as when your beloved announces that she has invited "the girls" and asks you to do the cooking. "Don't worry, Honey," she says. "It's just the girls!"

"How many of these 'girls' are there?" I ask.

"Just Lynn and Nancy and Michelle."

"But I barely know them," I protest.

"Don't worry, Honey. It's just the girls."

It's never "just the girls". It's always a group of successful, intelligent, attractive, single women whom you barely know. In this case, it's Lynn, Nancy, and Michelle. These are some of the women that constitute the highly secretive sub-culture known as "Marcie's Inner Circle". I'm pretty sure that the three of them along with Marcie constitute a quorum. These will be women who are analyzing your every move, every comment, how your hair looks, what kind of shoes you're wearing, and which wine you've chosen as though they would be required to give a high-level intelligence briefing as soon as you've left the room, which of course they are. If you make the slightest faux paus, they'll know it. You might as well start the bonfire and get out the torches for them, because you're bound to screw something up. It's unavoidable.

I could go on and on but, before I get myself kicked out of our social circle, let me say thank goodness Marcie's friends aren't like that - except for the fact that they're all incredibly successful, highly intelligent, unbelievably attractive, and usually single. They've also been very kind in their reviews of my cooking – especially my grilled lamb chops.

Serve the chops with Lima Beans Incognito.

For Turnin' and Burnin'

A man under pressure's best friend – his Grill
Grill Tongs
Chef's Knife
Butcher Knife
Measuring Spoons
Kitchen String
2 mixing Bowls
Corkscrew
Wine Glass

Ingredients

1 rack of lamb (8 bones) sliced into individual chops, excess fat removed
3 tbsp. olive oil
4 tbsp. Kalamata Olive Tapenade
4 tbsp. goat cheese
3 tbsp. fresh rosemary, finely chopped
Salt
Pepper

To Swill while you Grill

This is one of the tougher "swill while you grill" entries. If you ever needed a drink it would be now. But you have to be smart – remember, the inner circle is watching you. Impress their sensibilities with a glass of Syrah and hold off on the Zinfandel until dinner. Do not, under any circumstances, drink from the decanter until all of your guests have departed.

Preparation
- Preheat the grill to medium high heat.
- Combine the rosemary, olive oil in a bowl and mix well.
- In a second bowl mix the Tapenade and goat cheese.
- Spread the lamb chops out over a cutting board and cut a 1 inch pocket into the side of each chop.
- Rub the rosemary marinade over the each chop and inside the butterflied pockets.
- Stuff each pocket with 1 tbsp of the Tapenade and cheese mixture.
- Sprinkle salt and pepper on the chops and grill 4 to 5 minutes per side.

Grilled Rack of Lamb

Most of the time, I'll slice a rack of lamb into individual chops before grilling. Once in a while, I'll cut the rack in half and grill it as two pieces. This allows for several presentation options, one of which is serving the half racks over steamed vegetables such as green beans. Drizzle a red wine and black peppercorn reduction over the lamb before serving.

For Turnin' and Burnin'
Grill
Grill Tongs
Cutting Board
Chef's Knife
Measuring Cup
Measuring Spoons
1 Gallon Ziploc Bag
Large Bowl
Corkscrew
Wine Glass

Ingredients
½ cup dry red wine
3 tbsp. fresh rosemary, finely chopped
1 rack of lamb, excess fat removed
¼ cup Cabernet and Black Peppercorn Reduction
Salt
Pepper

To Swill while you Grill
You already have to open a bottle of Cab for the reduction and the marinade– you owe it to yourself to have a glass or two just to make sure that it's worthy of cooking with.

Preparation

- Combine the wine, rosemary, salt, and pepper in a bowl and mix well.
- Place the lamb racks into the Ziploc bag and pour the marinade into the bag.
- Seal the bag and refrigerate for 1 hour, turning bag frequently.
- Preheat grill to medium high heat.
- Place lamb on grill, fat side down, and grill for 2 minutes.
- Turn lamb over and grill for 2 minutes more.
- Turn lamb and grill on each side for 8 – 10 minutes or until internal temperature reaches 145 degrees for medium rare.
- Plate the lamb (I usually plate over a raft of steamed green beans or asparagus) and top with the Black Peppercorn Cabernet reduction.
- Serve immediately.

Death Row Lamb Tacos

Have you ever asked yourself what you would choose for dinner if you knew that it would be your last meal on earth? Suffice to say that I've asked myself this question many times, always with different foods and beverages being the resulting answer. Some days I think that I would like to have an enormous steak, some days lobster, still other days an enormous steak *and* lobster. Appetizers, entrees, sides, salads, and even beverages vary on my last meal list, but one dish remains constant. Lamb tacos, either as an appetizer, entrée, or dessert are always part of my imagined "Last Meal Menu"; ergo, the name Death Row Lamb Tacos.

For Turnin' and Burnin'

Cutting Board
Chef's Knife
12-inch Saucepan with lid
Kitchen Tongs
Measuring Cup
Measuring Spoons
Bottle Opener
Corkscrew
Wine Glass

Ingredients

2 tbsp. olive oil
2 lbs. boneless leg of lamb
1 tbsp. Adobo seasoning
2 cloves garlic, minced
4 Serrano peppers, diced
3 tbsp. cilantro, minced, plus additional whole cilantro leaves for garnish
½ onion, minced for garnish
Salt
8 flour tortillas
Black pepper
Salsa Roja

To Swill while you Grill

If it's your last meal on earth, you should drink whatever you wish and as much as you like. If you plan to keep on living, have a couple of beers while the lamb is cooking, then switch to a Syrah or Zin during dinner. If I'm having lamb tacos as an app, I'll stay with beer through the tacos, and then switch to wine with the entrée.

Preparation

- Sprinkle the lamb with the Adobo seasoning.
- Over medium high heat in a 12-inch saucepan, sear the lamb and serranos in the olive oil until the lamb is browned on all sides.
- Add the garlic and 2 cups of water to the saucepan, reduce heat to simmer, and cover.
- Adjust flavor as desired with salt and pepper.
- Simmer for 45 minutes or until lamb is cooked throughout and tender.
- Add cilantro and adjust seasonings to taste.
- Remove lamb to cutting board, allowing juices to remain in saucepan on low heat, uncovered.
- Shred the lamb using two forks.
- Return lamb to saucepan, mixing well with the reserved liquid and allow lamb to return to a simmer.
- Serve with heated tortillas and garnishes of pepper, whole cilantro leaves, and minced onions.

Pork

Bacon. Ham. Ribs. Pork roasts. "Bridges to Nowhere" added to federal legislation. Pork tenderloin. Carnitas. An almost endless variety of sausages. Pork is so good that companies make businesses out of using turkey to make healthier versions of the stuff. It shares much with lamb or beef in terms of its versatility, and it tastes great. What's more, it's generally a lot less expensive than red meat. When was the last time you ever heard of someone hosting a Cow Roast? People have pig roasts all the time. Think pig on a spit. Get some hula dancers, a Mai Tai and an apple and you have a luau. When we host a big party, pork is always a finalist, if not the winner, in our discussions of what to serve as a main course. That's why pork immediately came to mind when the "Danimal" and I decided to cook together one Sunday.

Dan is a fellow techno-geek that I met in Cleveland at the Stonebrook Driving Range and Sports Bar, which was located near both my office and hotel. He is a bright, no nonsense kind of guy that likes to eat and enjoys tipping back a few beers. When he gets a burr in his saddle, he can't rest until he figures out what to do about it.

Stonebrook, in order to give its cook a day off each week, doesn't serve food on Sundays. The bar and range are open but the kitchen is closed. They do, however, have a charcoal grill on their enormous outdoor patio that overlooks the range. Surrounded by trees, the range is one of the prettiest and most serene looking locations in the area, and it is not uncommon to see deer walking lazily across the range during the afternoon.

At some point during the summer, Dan convinced John, a PGA professional and Stonebrook's owner, to let him bring some sausages one Sunday and cook them on the grill. Dan foreseeing what was likely to happen, and seeing the hungry jealous eyes of everyone else on the patio, cooked enough to share with everyone. This was the beginning of the Sunday cookout at Stonebrook. (Except for one Sunday when John let me use the kitchen and I did Italian day, complete with apps, pasta, bread, and 12 quart stockpot of red sauce, most of the Sunday cooking was done outside on the grill.)

Others took turns bringing food and cooking, but usually it was Dan at the grill. When September came, the Sunday cookout became the Sunday tailgate party. As more and more people learned of the (almost) weekly cookout, folks would bring salads and desserts. John would move the big screen television out onto the patio and we'd all eat and watch the Browns game.

Leading up to one weekend when I was planning to stay in town, I spoke to John and asked if I could plan the Sunday menu and use his kitchen to do some prep work and sides. After getting John's okay, and his agreement to comp all of Dan's and my drinks for the day, I approached Dan.

"I'll get the food and do the stuff in the kitchen if you'll do the grilling," I said.

"Fine by me – as long as they don't run out of beer," Dan replied.

By this point, the tailgate party was averaging twenty or so people on a regular basis. I tend to overestimate on food buying and it was a good thing in this case.

On Saturday morning before the cookout, for kicks, I decided to take the menu a little upscale. We picked up whole beef tenderloin, whole pork tenderloin, flank steak, a whole turkey, chicken breasts, Italian sausages, kielbasa, and bratwursts along with all of the produce and other items that we would need.

At 11:30am on Sunday, as we were in the middle of prep work, (I think that I was cutting the turkey into pieces at this point) about 20 guys walked in to have their mid-season fantasy football league supplemental draft and trade session. I don't know much about fantasy football but I do know this – those guys could drink. And with all of the activity going on in the kitchen, they were looking forward to eating as well.

In the end, between the fantasy football guys and the regulars, we had about fifty people for the party that day. Thank goodness John went out and bought an additional whole beef tenderloin. In addition to salads and desserts, we served all of the sausages, black pepper crusted whole pork tenderloin (sliced) with salsa verde, Prosciutto and provolone flank steak pinwheels, turkey and chicken glazed in a southern mustard based barbeque sauce, and sliced grilled beef tenderloin with a raspberry zinfandel reduction. From what I understand, almost two years later people are still talking about the food from that day.

Grilled Black Pepper Crusted Whole Pork Tenderloin

Sometimes I can't decide whether I like pork tenderloin more for its taste of for the versatility of the leftovers. If you have leftover pork, shredding it and mixing with barbeque sauce makes a fantastic sandwich. Try chopping the pork and incorporating it into an omelet with chiles and onions for a Mexican morning twist.

First things first, though. Once I grill the whole loin, I'll typically slice it into ½ inch pieces and serve with either Salsa Verde or a fruit salsa (think mango, peach, or papaya). Grilled peaches make a nice compliment. At parties, the sliced pork also goes well with small browned rolls for sandwiches. I like to serve the salsas on the side as opposed to spooning over the entire dish.

For Turnin' and Burnin'
Your handy, dandy Grill
Large Mixing Bowl
Chef's Knife
Measuring Cup
Measuring Spoons
Cutting Board
Instant Read Meat Thermometer
Carving Board
Carving Knife

Ingredients
3 cloves fresh garlic, minced
4 tbsp. olive oil
4 tbsp. rosemary, minced
½ cup onion, finely chopped
2 tbsp. kosher salt
Black pepper
1 whole pork tenderloin, cleaned of excess fat and all silver skin
2 beers to drink during the cooking process

To Swill while you Grill

Pinot Noir is a super match for grilled pork, so decant a bottle to have with dinner. In the meantime, drink beer with your friends who are hovering around your grill waiting for the opportunity to give you cooking advice.

Preparation

- Mix first 5 ingredients together in a large bowl.
- Add the whole tenderloin to the bowl and cover the tenderloin in the marinade.
- Cover the bowl and refrigerate for at least 1 hour.
- Preheat grill to 375 degrees.
- Rub black pepper over the entire loin, creating a light crust.
- Find a friend that likes to drink beer while talking about wine, grab a couple of beers, and debate whether you think red or white wine goes better with pork. (They both do).
- Grill the tenderloin, turning frequently until the temperature in the center of the pork reaches 165 degrees on an instant read meat thermometer.
- Remove tenderloin from grill and tent with foil on a carving board for 15 minutes.
- Carve into ½ inch slices, arrange on a large platter, and serve.

Smoky, Spicy Ribs with a Buzz

Ribs are the source of more cooking debates than any other grillable protein than I can think of. Beef versus pork. St. Louis versus Kansas City. Hickory versus mesquite wood. Vinegar based sauce versus tomato-based sauce versus mustard-based sauce. Sweet versus spicy. Hot and fast versus low and slow.

I like my ribs on the spicy side and cooked to the point where they're tender, but have a little "pull" to them. I want the meat to come off of the bone easily when eaten, but not to the point where the meat is falling off of the bone by itself. You know, where you have to tug just a little.

Remember though, it's about how you like your ribs, not how some guy writing a cookbook likes ribs. As always, experiment with time, temperature, and spice.

For Turnin' and Burnin'

Your Handy, Dandy Grill
Small Pan for wood chips
Small Mixing Bowl
Chef's Knife
Measuring Cup
Measuring Spoons
Aluminum Foil
Cutting Board
Carving Board
Grill Brush

Ingredients

1 tbsp. cayenne pepper
1 tbsp. paprika
1 tsp. onion salt
1 tsp. black pepper
1 tsp. kosher salt
1 tsp. cumin
1 tsp. celery salt
3 racks of baby back or St. Louis ribs (racks halved)
2 cups wood chips (hickory or mesquite)
White wine vinegar
½ cup apple juice
½ cup dark rum
¼ cup yellow mustard
¼ cup ketchup
¼ cup A1 Sauce
1 tbsp. Tabasco sauce
1 tbsp. honey or molasses (optional)
1 cooler full of beer on ice

To Swill while you Grill

These ribs are going to take you about 5 ½ hours to get just right. I would recommend going with a light American picnic beer (i.e., Miller Lite) during the cooking process so that you aren't slurring your words over a dinner. With dinner, you'll want to consider a spicy red, like Syrah, that will stand up to the spice in the rub.

Preparation

- To make your rub, mix first 7 ingredients together in a medium small bowl.
- Rinse the ribs and dry with a paper towel. Trim any big pieces of excess fat (unless you like big pieces of excess fat).
- Apply the spice rub to the ribs with your hands, place ribs on a large platter, cover, and refrigerate.
- Wash your hands. The last thing you want to deal with is rubbing your eyes and then experiencing the joy of cayenne pepper coming in contact with your cornea.
- Preheat grill to 350 degrees.
- Place wood chips into a pan and cover with water. Place pan on grill. (There are two kinds of people in this world. Some like to soak the wood chips ahead of time for 30 minutes, drain the water, and then place the pan of wet chips on the grill. I'm not one of those people.)
- Cook ribs, about 10 minutes per side, then turn grill down to low heat (about 225 degrees) and smoke ribs, turning every 30 minutes for 2 hours. While the ribs are cooking over low heat, make a "mop" of ½ cup of vinegar and ½ cup of water. Brush the ribs with this mop and then again each time that you turn them.
- Now is a good time to check to make sure the beers in your cooler are all getting along

with each other. Grab the coldest one that you can find because his icy personality is not appreciated by the others. Repeat process throughout the afternoon.

- Once the ribs have cooked for 2 hours or so, they should have gotten the benefit of the smoking wood chips. In a measuring cup, combine the apple juice and dark rum, stirring until mixed well.
- Place each half rack of ribs on a sheet of aluminum foil that is large enough to cover the ribs when closed.
- Carefully pour the rum and apple juice mixture over each rack of ribs.
- Wrap the ribs up in the foil and return to the grill.
- Cook for another hour, then turn the packages and cook for 1 hour more.
- While the foil-wrapped ribs are cooking, combine the ketchup, mustard, A1 sauce, and Tabasco to make your barbecue sauce.
- Remove the ribs from the foil and return to the grill.
- I like a little sauce on my ribs; you may like more, none, or your sauce on the side. Any way works. If you plan to sauce your ribs, now's the time to do it. Brush sauce on ribs, turn and sauce the other side. The goal here is to let the sauce caramelize on the ribs, but not burn. 10 – 15 minutes per side should do nicely.
- Once saucing is complete, remove ribs to a carving board and tent with aluminum foil. Let rest for 10 minutes.
- Serve as half racks or cut ribs into smaller portions (3 bones works for me).

Spicy Pulled Pork (Carnitas)

Carnitas (spicy pork) may well be the junction at which Mexico and South Carolina (or anywhere else that y'all is spoken) meet on the way to culinary heaven. All of the pig pickin' goodness of pulled pork and all of the spiciness of Mexican seasoning and chiles come together in this dish. Think soccer-match-meets-tailgate-party. The only dilemma is whether to serve the pork on tortillas or a bun. Use the leftovers as the pork component of Cuban sandwiches or reheat and serve as a breakfast meat in place of sausage or bacon.

For Turnin' and Burnin'
That big old Oven that we so rarely use in this cookbook
Large Mixing Bowl
Chef's Knife
Measuring Cup
Measuring Spoons
Cutting Board
Instant Read Meat Thermometer
Carving Board
Carving Knife
Cooler with Ice
1 cross-cultural friend (optional)

Ingredients
2 tbsp. olive oil
3 lb. Boston Butt pork roast
4 jalapeños, seeds removed and chopped
1 medium onion cut into 6 wedges
2 tbsp. Adobo Seasoning
2 tbsp. garlic powder
Salt
Black pepper

To Swill while you Grill
Canned or bottled beer out of the cooler works well while preparing the pork. Put the cooler out on the patio. This will give you an opportunity to get out of the kitchen and give your guests somewhere other than the kitchen to hang out while you're trying to cook.

Preparation
- Preheat oven to 375 degrees.
- Sprinkle 1 tsp. or Adobo seasoning, 1 tsp. of powdered garlic, and a sprinkling of salt and pepper over the pork.
- Over medium high-heat on the stovetop, heat the olive oil, and then add the pork roast.
- Sear the pork until lightly browned on all sides, about 10 minutes total.
- Add 2 cups of water, the onion, and jalapeños to a baking dish.
- Add the pork and sprinkle the remaining Adobo and garlic powder.
- Cook the pork in the oven for 1 hours, then reduce heat to 250 degrees and cook for 3 ½ hours more, basting the pork with its juices and turning every 30 minutes or until the center of the pork is 175 degrees when checked with a meat thermometer.
- If you've invited your cross-cultural friend, grab those beers and debate the relative merits of soccer versus American football. If you don't have any friends, drink both of the beers yourself and resolve to get out more and meet people.
- Once the pork is done, remove from the oven and set the baking dish on the stovetop. Do not discard the juice, as you will need it later.
- Using a pair of tongs, remove the pork from the baking dish and place on a cutting board.
- Cut the pork into ½ inch slices and shred using two forks. Discard any large pieces of fat as you go.
- Return the shredded pork to the baking dish, making sure to cover the pork in its juices, return to oven for 10 minutes, and then let rest for 5 minutes.
- Using a slotted spoon, and depending on who won the football-soccer debate, spoon the pork onto tortillas or buns.
- If serving on tortillas, serve with salsa (red or green) or Pico de Gallo. If serving on buns, a little chopped onion makes a nice addition.

Bill Allen

Cuban Sandwich

During my non self-imposed retirement, I've tried to be productive with my time. The first couple of months were easy. As we were in the final ten weeks before our wedding, I took on the job of "Accidental Wedding Planner," creating spreadsheets, mailing invitations, and running errands for Marcie, and doing whatever other one-off wedding tasks that came up. I added these responsibilities to my burgeoning portfolio of distance running, dog walking, and cooking tasks and had enough to keep me out of trouble for a while.

The difficult thing about cooking for a prospective bride is that you may starve to death if you follow her diet. That was the case in our house anyway.

"Whaddaya feel like for lunch today, Honey?" I would ask.

"I don't think I want anything. I had 4 almonds and a non-fat Chai Latte for breakfast. I'm fine, thanks!," Marcie would reply.

"Sweetie, that was 5 hours ago. You need to have something," I would say.

"I have to fit into my wedding dress," she would say.

"If you die of starvation, you're not going to look your best on our wedding day," I say.

"Okay, how about a little sandwich or something?"

"Sure," I would say, relieved that I would finally get to have some lunch. (Everyone knows that you can't have lunch in front of a dieting bride-to-be unless she is eating as well).

I took the little sandwich request and figured that to mean that I could make anything that I wanted – as long as it could be wrapped between two pieces of bread. This Cuban sandwich lets you have two different types of pork in the same meal. To prepare the roast pork component, use my Carnitas recipe. Press the sandwiches with a small stockpot while heating the bread in a frying pan. I prefer not to use a Panini press for two reasons. First, a Panini press does not heat the bread evenly. Second, Cuban sandwiches don't have ridges in them.

For Turnin' and Burnin'
Bread Knife
Cutting Board
Large Saucepan
2-quart Saucepot
Corkscrew
Wineglass

Ingredients (for each sandwich)
3 oz. roasted pork, shredded (see Carnitas recipe)
3 thin slices of ham
2 thin slices of Swiss cheese
4 sandwich dill pickle slices
Yellow mustard
8" loaf of Cuban or French bread

To Swill while you Grill
Have a glass of Spanish Rioja while preparing Cuban sandwiches. Have the rest of the bottle while eating the sandwiches and daydreaming about cigars that you can't legally get your hands on in the U.S.

Preparation

- Preheat a burner on the stovetop to medium heat.
- Square off the ends of the bread.
- Slice the bread almost completely in half, as you would do for making a sandwich.
- Spread mustard on both sides of the bread.
- Add the ham, then the pork.
- Top with the Swiss cheese and then the pickles.
- Place the whole sandwich in a large frying pan over the heat and press the sandwich down with a small stockpot for 20 seconds.
- Turn the sandwich over and press for an additional 20 seconds.
- Slice diagonally to create two triangular halves and serve..

Poultry

When you live in a condo, you don't have any control of who your neighbors are. You also don't have to do yard work, but that's another discussion.

In both Chicago and Florida, we're privileged to have some of the best neighbors that anyone could ask for. We share Fourth of July and Labor Day cookouts with Janis and Jerry and Maria and Craig in Chicago and wintertime cocktail hours and dinner parties in Florida with Ron and Linda and Hugh and Jacquie. Because all of us like to entertain, weekends and holidays become a merry-go-round of visiting each other and sharing food and fun.

With our Florida friends, I believe that the Caribbean word for what we do most is "liming". Liming means that you're just hanging out for no particular reason without an agenda. After a hard days work, - for those poor souls in our group who actually *work*- a little liming is just what the doctor ordered. Have a few cocktails, throw some chicken breasts on the grill, have a few more cocktails, then eat. That's liming.

Prosciutto and Swiss Cheese Stuffed Chicken Breasts

For many years, economics dictated that I would be subjected to some form of ground beef or chicken as part of my dinner at least five days each week. Sometime after feeling the initial urges to start clucking instead of speaking, things took a turn for the better and I abstained from eating chicken for a while. After about two years, and as my cholesterol level approached a perfect bowling score, my doctor said that I might want to reconsider my position on fowl. Since I wanted to be around to see my boys grow up, I decided to listen – just this once.

The goal became finding ways to prepare chicken and other poultry in a way that made my fowl seem less foul. So I decided to make a game out of it.

Why did the chicken cross the road?

Because I was chasing him so that I could make chicken breasts stuffed with Prosciutto and Swiss cheese.

Topped with Classic Hollandaise Sauce, it's my deconstruction of Chicken Cordon Bleu.

For Turnin' and Burnin'
The "Old Flamethrower" (grill)
Large Mixing Bowl
Chef's Knife
Cutting Board
Measuring Cup
Measuring Spoon
Grill Tongs
Corkscrew
Wineglass

Ingredients
½ cup Italian dressing for marinade
4 boneless, skinless chicken breasts, washed

4 slices Prosciutto de Parma
½ cup Classic Hollandaise Sauce
2 tbsp. chopped rosemary
4 pieces of Swiss cheese cut into 1 inch by 2 inch by ½ inch slices
1 tbsp. black pepper

To Swill while you Grill

Chicken, like pork, is a versatile partner for wine. I tend to base my choice of red versus white on the temperature outside. If I'm grilling in the cold, I'll have a Pinot Noir or Barbera. If it's a hot summer day, a crisp Sav Blanc makes a good swilling wine.

Preparation

- Cut a 3-inch slice into the side of each chicken breast to make a pocket for the stuffing.
- In a large bowl, cover the chicken with the half of the Italian dressing and the black pepper making sure to marinate the inside of the pockets.
- Cover and refrigerate for 30 minutes.
- Preheat grill to 350 degrees.
- Wrap a slice of Prosciutto around each slice of cheese and stuff these into the chicken breasts.
- Press the chopped rosemary onto the marinated chicken breasts.
- Grill the chicken breasts for 3 minutes on each side.
- Reduce grill heat to low (or, if grilling over charcoal move to a cooler spot on the grill) and cook for 5 minutes per side or until juices run clear.
- Top with the Hollandaise sauce and serve.

Axis of Chicken Parmesan

I've been known to catch a little grief about the amount of sausage and red meat that I consume. Italian red sauce is one of the many ways to turn a chicken breast into a guilty pleasure. I call this "Axis of Chicken Parmesan" because it brings together those old World War II buddies – Italian red sauce, German beer, and Japanese breadcrumbs. Serve this over boiled pasta with garlic bread.

For Turnin' and Burnin'

Large Saucepan
Measuring Spoon
12" Sauté Pan
Tongs
Chef's Knife
Cutting Board
Mixing Bowl
Baking Dish
Corkscrew
Wine Glass

Ingredients

2 cups liquid from Red Headed Red Sauce or other red pasta sauce
4 boneless, skinless chicken breasts
1 cup Parmesan cheese, shredded
Panko breadcrumbs
1 egg, beaten
4 tbsp. olive oil
Garlic powder
Salt
Pepper

To Swill while you Grill

While you're cooking, why not enjoy a Spaten (Munich) Lager? Besides, I needed a German beer to round out the whole "Axis" thing. Dinner will be the perfect time to enjoy a wine whose name ends in a vowel. Think Sangiovese, Chianti, Barbera, Amarone.

Preparation

- Preheat oven to 350 degrees.
- Evenly spread the sauce into a 9" x 13" x 2" baking dish.
- Dip each of the chicken breasts into the egg wash, then lightly coat in the breadcrumbs.
- In a large saucepan, over medium-high heat, heat the olive oil.
- Brown the chicken in the olive oil until crispy, about 3 minutes per side.
- Transfer the chicken to the baking dish, cover with more sauce and bake for 25 minutes.
- Remove from the oven and top with grated Parmesan cheese.
- Return to oven and bake for 5 minutes or until sauce is hot and cheese is melted.
- Serve over pasta with garlic bread.

Lemon-Rosemary Roasted Chicken with Vegetables

I remember having take-out Lemon Chicken from a Chinese restaurant as a teenager and thinking that it was the best chicken that I had ever eaten. When I applied the theory that lemons and chickens should spend more time together, roasted chicken seemed like a good place to start. Rubbing the lemon, rosemary, and butter spread under the skin of the chicken allows its flavor to permeate throughout the dish. Chunks of onions, potatoes, and carrots round out this classic Sunday dinner.

For Turnin' and Burnin'
Chef's Knife
Cutting Board
Measuring Cup
Measuring Spoon
Baking Dish or Roasting Pan
Turkey Baster
Aluminum Foil
Carving Board
Corkscrew
Wineglass

Ingredients
3 to 4 lb. whole chicken, washed
2 large potatoes cut into 1 inch chunks
2 carrots cut into 1 inch chunks
1 onion, halved and cut into wedges
2 sprigs plus 1 tbsp fresh chopped rosemary
4 oz. butter, softened
1 lemon halved plus 2 tbsp lemon juice
Salt
Black pepper

To Swill while you Grill
Sauvignon Blanc is a favorite quaff while on basting duty. The citrus notes of many Sav Blancs pair quite nicely with the lemon in the chicken recipe.

Preparation
- Preheat Oven to 350 degrees.
- In a medium bowl, mix the butter, chopped rosemary, and lemon juice by until well blended and creamy.
- Rub the lemon-butter-herb spread between the skin and meat of the chicken. If the skin tears a little, it won't be the end of the world, I promise.
- Pour two cups of water in a baking dish or roasting pan and place the chicken in the center of the dish or pan.
- Place the onions, carrots, and potatoes around the chicken.
- Cook for thirty minutes, and then baste the chicken with the juices from the pan. Repeat basting every fifteen minutes until chicken is browned and internal temperature is 170 degrees on an instant read thermometer.
- Remove from heat and let chicken rest, tented in foil, for 10 minutes on a carving board. Carve and serve with the vegetables.

Bill Allen
Roasted Turkey Breast

I owe a lot to the delicatessens of this world. They have provided me with endless hours of lunchtime joy and, other than a certain brewery in Boston, have ruined more of my diets than anything else I can think of. They can be expensive as well.

One thing you can do to save a little cash and still "get your sandwich on" is to roast turkey for your sandwiches at home. You'll have the freedom to spice it up however you like in addition to stashing some extra beer money away at the same time.

For Turnin' and Burnin'
Chef's Knife
Cutting Board
Measuring Cup
Measuring Spoon
Kitchen Tongs
Baking Dish or Roasting pan
Turkey Baster
Aluminum Foil
Carving Board
Bottle Opener

Ingredients
3 lb. turkey breast, rinsed and patted dry
2 tbsp. olive oil
3 tbsp. fresh rosemary, chopped
1 onion, cut into wedges
Salt
Black Pepper

To Swill while you Grill
If I'm yearning for the deli days, I'll drink one of those lagers from Boston while basting the turkey. If the diet police are after me, I'll have a glass of Pinot Noir instead.

Preparation
- Preheat Oven to 350 degrees.
- In a medium bowl, mix the olive oil, rosemary, ½ tsp of salt, and tsp of black pepper.
- Rub the mixture all over the turkey breast.
- Place the turkey breast in baking dish, then add 2 cups of water and the onion wedges. Sprinkle additional salt and black pepper onto turkey breast.
- Cook the turkey in the oven, basting at least every 30 minutes, turning at 45 minutes, for 1½ hours or until the internal temperature at the thickest part of the breast reaches 170 degrees on an instant read meat thermometer.
- Remove from oven and discard the onions and pan juices (unless you need them to make a gravy).
- Let the turkey stand for 15 minutes. Thinly carve to serve on sandwiches.

Seafood

Growing up in South Florida, some of my fondest childhood memories are of fishing trips with Papa Allen, my dad's father. We'd hop in his AMC Rebel and go "over yonder". Sometimes Grandmaw Allen would go with us. Other times it would just be the two of us, driving along the canal banks until we determined that we had reached the perfect spot. These were also the trips where Papa taught me to drive and chew tobacco at nine years old. Funny, my mom never got after him about the driving, but she nearly killed him over the "Great Chewing Tobacco Scandal of 1973".

Over yonder could have been to any of the canal banks near my hometown but the routine was always the same. We'd pick up some bait, head to the canal, fish for a while, and go to an outdoor vegetable market to buy a watermelon soda out of the machine. We'd then take our catch of pathetically small bream back to his house where he'd clean them. "Maw" would bread them and we'd fry them in lard on his Coleman outdoor gas stove. I remember Maw breading even the tiniest of fish because I would insist that they were big enough to eat.

About ten years later, I was introduced to crabbing and deep-sea fishing by my mother's uncles. Besides learning that fishing on a party boat does not mean that you should try to drink all of the beer in the first hour, I found that catching big fish was a lot more fun than catching small fish. It was also my first experience being far enough out on the ocean that I couldn't see land in any direction.

I've always loved fishing and perhaps that's part of the reason that I enjoy fresh seafood as much as I do. The year that we met, Marcie took me to Key West to celebrate my birthday weekend. If that were not enough, she chartered a 42' fishing boat with a Captain and First Mate for a 4-hour deep-sea fishing trip. Given that the staff equaled the number of guests, all I had to do was have a few adult beverages and fish. If you can call it fishing. I sat in an enormous swiveling chair and waited for a bite on one of the seven outrigger lines that were set up and tended to by the first mate. After 2 hours and several beers though, we hadn't had a single bite.

The captain came down from the boat's tower and asked, "You wanna catch some fish"?

"Absolutely," I said. "Isn't that the idea"?

"Well, I know of a wreck pretty close to here where I'm sure we'll hit some barracuda," he replied.

"Let's do it," I said.

Within 15 minutes of casting near the wrecked ship, I was able to haul in three 'cudas. Each one was about three feet long, and if you've never seen one up close, the teeth on these guys are even nastier in person than in photographs.

As we started back toward Key West, there was a hit on the line and the first mate moved the deep-sea fishing rod for that line into the holder in the swivel chair. About two minutes later he yelled, "Sail on the line."

I started reeling as fast as I could. Then the most amazing thing happened. The sailfish broke the surface and leapt several feet into the air, about fifty feet away from the boat. I reeled faster and faster. After about thirty minutes of fighting to get this fish in, the first mate reached over the side of the boat and hauled a 6 ½ - 7 foot sailfish out of the water for a picture. The captain estimated the weight at about 60 pounds. Who am I to argue?

After releasing the sailfish, we continued back to port. Before we arrived, however, we had one more hit on a line. This time it was a black fin tuna. Not as much of a fight as the sail but much, much tastier. He weighed in at 15 pounds, nine ounces, just about the amount of fish Marcie and I were ready to eat at this point.

We took half of our cleaned tuna, compliments of the first mate, to a local restaurant who paid us by the pound for the meat, then used it to make our dinner. It's the only time that I've eaten tuna sashimi and tuna steak that I've caught myself. It may or may not have been the best tuna dinner in the history of the world, but it was without a doubt one of the freshest.

Black Pepper and Sesame Crusted Seared Tuna Sashimi

There was quite a debate between the left and right sides of my brain as to whether I should include this recipe in the appetizer or seafood sections of this book. The seafood section won because, after that last story, you may be hungry for tuna.

This dish is easy, minimalist, and delicious on its own as an appetizer or perched on a bed of arugula with peach slices and a ginger-soy dressing.

For Turnin' and Burnin'
Sauté Pan
Chef's Knife
Cutting Board
Measuring Spoon
Kitchen Tongs
Bottle Opener
Shot Glass

Ingredients
6 oz. fresh tuna steak
2 tbsp. low sodium soy sauce
2 tbsp. sesame oil
3 tbsp. sesame seeds
2 tsp. black pepper
Sprigs of cilantro for garnish
4 oz. arugula
Additional soy sauce for dipping
Wasabi mustard

To Swill while you Grill
If you like Sake, here's a really good opportunity to enjoy some. Even better - pour the Sake into a shot glass and follow it with a bottle of Kirin lager.

Preparation

- Rub soy sauce over the tuna and refrigerate for 20 minutes.
- Over medium-high heat, add the sesame oil to a sauté pan.
- Rub the black pepper evenly over the tuna.
- Coat the tuna steak in sesame seeds pressing lightly to ensure that the seeds stick to the meat.
- Sear the tuna for about 1 minute per side or until lightly charred.
- Remove tuna and rest on a cutting board about 2 minutes.
- Slice tuna widthwise into ¼ inch strips.
- Arrange on a serving platter over arugula with the Additional soy sauce and Wasabi mustard.
- Garnish with the cilantro sprigs and serve.

Mahi Mahi Tacos

Whenever I hear a word repeated, I figure it must be important enough that I should pay attention to find out what all the fuss is about. "Verily, verily" was a big one growing up in church. "Chug! Chug!" was often heard a few years later. "_Mangia, mangia_" (Italian for "eat, eat!") is without a doubt my favorite.

Mahi Mahi tacos are a healthy dining option for those of you who care about such things; however, if healthy eating is not your bag, relax! They are a favorite lunch option of mine because they taste so good!

Sear some chunks of Mahi, heat up a few tortillas, and top with some Pico de Gallo for a quick and delicious change of pace.

For Turnin' and Burnin'

Sauté Pan
Large Skillet
Chef's Knife
Cutting Board
Measuring Spoon
Mixing Bowl
Kitchen Tongs
Margarita Glass

Ingredients

8 oz. fresh Mahi Mahi, cut into 1-inch chunks
2 tbsp. olive oil
1 tbsp. fresh thyme
1 tsp. cayenne pepper
1 tsp. black pepper
Salt
2 tbsp cilantro, chopped
Flour tortillas
Pico de Gallo

To Swill while you Grill
Since you're behaving yourself by eating fish tacos, you should reward yourself with a Margarita. If, like me, you don't have to worry about going back to work after lunch, have two Margaritas.

Preparation
- Combine the thyme, cayenne pepper, and black pepper in a mixing bowl.
- Coat the fish in the spice mixture.
- Heat the olive oil in a sauté pan over medium high.
- Preheat a dry skillet to high heat.
- Cook the fish in the olive oil, turning often, until all sides are browned and fish is cooked through, about 9 minutes. Remember that the skillet next to the sauté pan is hot! Don't burn yourself.
- When the fish has about 2 minutes remaining to cook, begin heating the tortillas in the skillet. The tortillas should only need to cook for 20 seconds on each side.
- Fill the warm tortillas with the fish and serve with Pico de Gallo and cilantro.

Vera Cruz Red Snapper (Huachinango Veracruzana)
I have a special place in my heart (and taste buds) for Mexican food. Having lived there for six years, I had the good fortune to experience Mexico's food prepared in all of its tradition and glory. It was quite a learning experience as well. For instance, you may receive strange looks if you were to order a beef enchilada in Mexico City. In traditional Mexican cooking, enchiladas are normally thought of to be made with chicken. Who knew? And those little half moon hard taco shells that I grew up with? Nope. Not to worry though. Given the choice between the more innovative and traditional approaches to Mexican cooking, I'll take the traditional versions of these dishes almost every time. One exception to this is my take on Vera Cruz Red Snapper. I mainly stay true to the traditional ingredients but have made a couple of changes, the most noteworthy being the replacement of Chile Guajillo with Serrano peppers. If you cannot find red snapper, Coho or Lane snapper are wonderful alternatives. I've also made this with Tilapia when snapper was not available. I often serve the snapper alongside black beans over yellow rice. To dress the dish up even more, sometimes I'll top each sautéed each filet with 2 or 3 Tequila Lime Shrimp. I finished the dish this way for the first time when preparing for Jan and Jim, and it was a huge hit.

For Turnin' and Burnin'
12" Sauté Pan
Chef's Knife
Medium Bowl (for egg wash)
Cutting Board
Measuring Spoon
Kitchen Tongs
Corkscrew
Wine glass

Ingredients

3 tbsp. olive oil

10 small spring onions, chopped into ¼ inch pieces (or sliced into fine rings if using spring onions)

2 garlic cloves, minced

2 Serrano peppers, seeded and chopped into ¼ inch pieces

4 red snapper filets, thoroughly washed.

1 egg, beaten

Panko bread crumbs

2 large ripe tomatoes, seeded and chopped into ½ inch cubes

Juice of 2 limes

Kosher salt

Black pepper

5 oz. manzanilla olives, sliced and drained

3 ½ oz. capers, drained

4 tbsp. fresh cilantro, finely chopped

To Swill while you Grill

A good way to kill a bottle of Chablis is to have a glass while you're getting your tools and ingredients out, another glass while preparing dinner, two glasses with dinner, and whatever's left in the bottle while you clear the table. This, of course, assumes that no one else in your dinner party is sharing the Chablis with you.

Preparation

- Over medium-high heat, add the olive oil to a 12" sauté pan.
- Add the onions, garlic, and Serrano peppers, heating and gently stirring until the onions are translucent, about 5 minutes.
- Dip each of the snapper filets in the egg wash
- Salt and pepper the filets, then lightly coat with Panko breadcrumbs. "Lightly coat" is the operative phrase here. We're going for a crispy finish, not Aunt Maybelle's fried chicken. Be careful to press the breadcrumbs onto the fish to ensure that they stick to the fish during cooking.
- Carefully place each filet into the sauté pan. Some of the onions, garlic, and peppers will attach to the breading on the fish. (This is a good thing!)
- Add the juice of 1 lime and cook for 4 to 5 minutes.
- Gently turn the filets taking care not to tear the breading.
- Add the juice of the remaining lime.
- Fold in the tomatoes, olives, and capers and cook 4 minutes more.
- Sprinkle in the Cilantro.
- Add salt and pepper to taste.
- Plate each of the snapper filets.
- Sauté the remaining vegetable mixture for 30 seconds and spoon it onto the fish.

Crab and Shrimp Stuffed Tilapia

Here's a fun way to liven up baked tilapia. By rolling the fish around the stuffing that you make, you will build contrasts in flavor and texture. Plate the fish over a raft of green beans or asparagus for a visually appealing presentation. Any leftover stuffing can be used to make Shrimp 'n Crab Cakes. Pair the stuffed tilapia with Sauvignon Blanc.

For Turnin' and Burnin'
12" Sauté Pan
Chef's Knife
Medium Bowl (for egg wash)
Cutting Board
Mixing Bowl
Measuring Spoon
Baking Dish
Corkscrew
Wine Glass

Ingredients
3 tbsp. olive oil
6 oz. white crab meat
8 shrimp, washed, deveined, and cut into thirds
2 spring onions, diced
1 celery stick, diced
1 jalapeño, diced
2 tsp. fresh thyme
½ cup dry white wine
2 tbsp. prepared horseradish
¼ cup cream cheese, at room temperature
6 Tilapia filets
2 tbsp. Panko bread crumbs
Juice of 2 limes
Kosher salt
Black pepper
Toothpicks

To Swill while you Grill
Sometimes I think Marcie would drink Sav. Blanc with a peanut butter sandwich, but in this case, I must agree. The acidity of the wine pairs fabulously with the flavors in the fish.

Preparation
- Over medium-high heat, add the olive oil to a 12" sauté pan.
- Add the onions, celery, and jalapeños, heating and gently stirring until the onions are translucent, about 3 minutes.
- Add the crab, shrimp, thyme, and ¼ cup of the white wine and continue sautéing for 4 minutes more.

- Add salt and pepper to taste.
- Remove crab/shrimp mixture from heat and transfer to a mixing bowl.
- Add the breadcrumbs, horseradish, and cream cheese and stir until thoroughly combined.
- Spoon mixture onto tilapia filets.
- Preheat oven to 400 degrees.
- Carefully roll up each filet and secure with toothpicks.
- Place the filets in a baking dish and top with the remaining wine and lime juice.
- Sprinkle salt and pepper to taste over each filet.
- Bake the fish for 12-15 minutes.
- Remove toothpicks from each filet and serve.

Panko Crusted Pompano Filets

Have I mentioned that I adore fish? Well there's no fish that I love more than Florida Pompano. It has a sweet delicate flavor that makes it unique from any other fish that I've eaten.

Our Saturday morning vegetable market in the winter has the added bonus of having a seafood guy who often times has pompano for sale. He usually sells out early so, early in the season, we wake up before sunrise to make sure we arrive before all of the pompano is gone. Our guy sells it whole and, while it's wonderful grilled as a whole fish, we also like it filleted. (Marcie thinks that it's less intimidating that way). I like to precede this dish with a simple mixed salad and serve the pompano with steamed green beans.

For Turnin' and Burnin'
12" Sauté Pan
Chef's Knife
Medium Bowl (for egg wash)
Cutting Board
Mixing Bowl
Measuring Spoon
Baking Dish
Corkscrew
Wine Glass

Ingredients
3 tbsp. olive oil
10 small spring onions, sliced into fine rings
1 Serrano pepper, seeded and chopped into ¼ inch pieces
2 Pompano fillets, thoroughly washed.
1 egg, beaten
Panko bread crumbs
4 oz. white wine (I like to use Sauvignon Blanc for this recipe)
1 extra glass of white wine (I like to drink Sauvignon Blanc while cooking this recipe)
Juice of 2 limes
Kosher salt to taste

Bill Allen

Black pepper
3 ½ oz. capers, drained
4 tbsp. fresh cilantro, finely chopped

To Swill while you Grill
Any cocktail will do during the cooking phase; just make sure you pick a light white to pair during the eating phase. Anything heavy will overpower the subtle flavor of the fish.

Preparation
- Over medium-high heat, add the olive oil to a 12" sauté pan.
- Add the onions and Serrano peppers, heating and gently stirring until the onions are translucent, about 5 minutes.
- Dip each of the snapper filets in the egg wash
- Salt and pepper the pompano filets, then lightly coat with Panko breadcrumbs. (Remember my Aunt Maybelle comment in the previous recipe). Be careful to press the breadcrumbs onto the fish to ensure that they stick to the fish during cooking.
- Carefully place each filet into the sauté pan. Some of the onions and peppers will attach to the breading on the fish
- Add the juice of 1 lime and cook for 4 to 5 minutes.
- Add 2 oz. of the wine and gently turn the filets taking care not to tear the breading.
- Add the juice of the remaining lime.
- Sprinkle in the capers and cook 3 more minutes.
- Add the remaining white wine and cook 3 minutes more or until breading is golden brown.
- Sprinkle in the Cilantro.
- Add salt and pepper to taste.
- Serve immediately.

Scallops in Beurre Blanc
Seared scallops are so delicious that you'd think they would be more difficult to prepare. Adding a dusting of paprika and a Beurre Blanc (French for "white butter") sauce makes the finished product absolutely decadent. Serve over homemade sweet potato fries or grilled asparagus.

For Turnin' and Burnin'
2 Large Sauté Pans
Chef's Knife
Rubber Spatula
Cutting Board
Mixing Bowl
Measuring Spoon
Corkscrew
Wine Glass

Ingredients
5 tbsp. butter
3 tbsp. olive oil
2 tbsp. shallots, minced
2 strips of bacon
¼ cup white wine
1 lb. fresh (U15) scallops
1 tsp. cornstarch (optional)
Salt
Black pepper.
Paprika
Fresh thyme for garnish

To Swill while you Grill
Treating yourself to a glass of light white wine, like Pinot Grigio, will demonstrate your high level of sophistication and class to all of your guests. (I, on the other hand, already know your high level of sophistication and class because you're cooking this recipe!)

Preparation
- Over medium-high heat, add the bacon to one of the sauté pans.
- Cook until crisp, remove from heat and place bacon on paper towels to degrease and cool. Discard bacon grease.
- Once cool, crumble the bacon into small bits. Set aside.
- In the other sauté pan, melt 3 tbsp of butter.
- Add the scallops, white wine and shallots to the pan. Top each scallop with a dash of salt and pepper.
- Cook the scallops for 3 to 4 minutes per side, turning once.
- Once the shallots have cooked, remove them from the pan and set aside, keeping warm.
- Whisk the remaining butter and into the Beurre blanc that is in the sauté pan, adding cornstarch if necessary to thicken.
- Plate the scallops, then top with Beurre Blanc, a sprinkle of paprika, a little of the bacon crumbles, and thyme to garnish.

Colossal Shrimp Thermador
One day as I was enjoying my second adult beverage on the lanai, I became troubled about the cost of Lobster Thermador. To both my friend Mr. Woodford Reserve and me, it seemed that something that is as delicious as lobster should not require a second mortgage to finance. Now, before you start thinking that I failed freshman economics and have no concept of how the rules of supply and demand dictate the cost of lobster, please consider that it was Mr. Woodford who was in charge of logical thinking during this particular conversation.

We debated back and forth and, sometime during my third round of cocktails, it dawned on me that I could probably make do with colossal shrimp in place of the lobster. By butterflying the shrimp, stuffing them with a Thermador sauce, and baking, I could make dinner without having to sell plasma to pay for it.

Serve over yellow rice with a glass or two of Chardonnay.

For Turnin' and Burnin'
2 Medium Sauté Pans
Small Saucepot
Chef's Knife
Cutting Board
Mixing Bowl
Measuring Spoon
Baking Dish
Corkscrew
Wine Glass

Ingredients
1lb. colossal shrimp (11-15 count), peeled, deveined, and butterflied half way through
2 tbsp. olive oil
3 spring onions, sliced into fine rings
6 tbsp. all purpose flour
2 Serrano chiles, seeded and finely diced (optional)
5 tablespoons butter
2 oz. portabella mushroom stems, diced
1 tsp. paprika
½ cup milk
½ cup Asiago cheese, grated
Panko bread crumbs
¼ cup dry white wine
¼ cup Parmesan cheese, grated
Kosher salt to taste
Black pepper to taste
1 lemon, halved, then sliced for garnish

To Swill while you Grill
Out of respect of the origin of this recipe, I am required to have a Bourbon Manhattan while doing my prep work. With dinner, I make one of my rare pilgrimages to the Chardonnay bottle.

Preparation
- In a medium saucepan, over medium-high heat, sauté the onions, Serranos, and mushrooms in the olive oil. Cook for about 5 minutes or until the onions are tender and translucent.
- In a small saucepot, make a roux. To do this, heat 4 tbsp of the butter until melted, then whisk in the flour. When the roux starts bubbling, turn the heat down to simmer and cook for about 2 minutes more.
- Add the wine, milk, and finally the roux to the pan with the onions, mushrooms and

peppers and stir to blend well. Turn heat down to low and allow the sauce to thicken, stirring regularly.

- In a separate pan, sauté the shrimp and ½ tsp of paprika in the remaining 1 tbsp of butter until shrimp turns pink.
- Preheat oven to broil.
- Arrange the shrimp in a baking dish and carefully spoon in the Thermador mixture. Top with cheese, breadcrumbs and the remaining paprika.
- Broil for 5 minutes or until the cheese is bubbling and the breadcrumbs are toasted. Serve over yellow rice.

Melt Your Mouth Snapper over Jasmine Rice

I believe that there are very few absolutes in life and many shades of gray. One thing that I'm certain of, however, is the wisdom in finding a partner who has a similar predilection as oneself for spicy food. Unless you plan on going out for dinner for the rest of your lives whenever you are together, you need to have common ground relative to the level of heat that you incorporate into your cooking.

I am fortunate in this regard as Marcie enjoys spice and chilis at least as much as I do. This allows us to cook Asian and Latin American dishes to our taste, knowing that, if the cook likes the spice balance, the other most likely will as well.

If you plan to serve "Melt your Mouth Snapper" to guests, you'll want to know their sensitivity to heat before springing this one on them. To assist in the relaxation of your guests' spice detectors, a helping or two of Olive Soup is recommended before dinner. Serve the snapper over jasmine rice. I'll give you credit for not needing my help to cook rice. Follow the directions on the package. I prefer to have a beer with this meal, but if you insist on having wine, pair the snapper with a crisp white wine, like Viognier.

For Turnin' and Burnin'
2 Medium Sauté Pans
Small Saucepot
Chef's Knife
Cutting Board
Mixing Bowl
Measuring Spoon
Baking Dish
Corkscrew
Wine Glass

Ingredients
2 tbsp. olive oil
1 large onion, chopped
3 cloves garlic, minced
1 Habanero pepper, diced
1lb. red snapper filets cut into 1-inch chunks
4 cilantro sprigs
Soy sauce

To Swill while you Grill

Beer is a good choice while working in the kitchen. As you test the spice level in the sauce, you'll thank me (even if you do it silently). Serve with Viognier, but make sure to let your guests know that you have beer on ice, just in case.

Preparation

- In a wok, over medium-high heat, sauté the onions and garlic in the olive oil. Cook for about 5 minutes or until the onions are tender and translucent.
- Add the habaneros, snapper, cilantro sprigs and soy sauce and cook for about 4 minutes more, until fish is cooked on all sides and throughout.
- Discard the cilantro sprigs and serve divide evenly onto plates over jasmine rice.

Casseroles

The holidays are a special time for family, friends, fun, and food (not necessarily in that order). I am especially grateful to have friends and family who share my appreciation for food and have been such willing, if albeit unknowing, volunteers as I have tested my recipes over time.

When people think about the holiday season in the United States, generally, the first thing that comes to mind is the period between Thanksgiving Day and New Year's Day. In this five to six week period, depending on your point of view, there can be anywhere from two to seven holidays – Thanksgiving, Chanukah, Kwanzaa, Christmas Eve, Christmas Day, New Year's Eve and New Year's Day. Some people may choose other periods, the Lenten season is one that comes to mind, but most people agree that late November through the New Year constitute the "holiday season". I now have the greater understanding that the holiday season does not end with the Champagne toasts and college football games on New Year's Day but, rather, extends through the first weekend in February. This is because no holiday season (in our home, at least) is complete without paying homage to the single most important party event of the year – Marcie Gras.

Marcie Gras, not to be confused with Mardi Gras, Carnival, or Fat (Shrove) Tuesday, is loosely translated to mean, "It's Marcie's birthday so let's have a big, fat party"! It's a masquerade party, complete with an inflatable jester, music, food, dancing, and all of the fun that you would normally associate with a party for 50 people. Okay I can see how you might confuse this with one of those other pre-Lenten fests.

Like Curly, our ninety-pound (sub) standard poodle, Marcie Gras has been a part of our household for longer than I have. Marcie originally hosted this party around the time of her birthday in order to get together with her girlfriends and drink wine and hang out. Eventually boys were invited, apparently because these ladies needed someone to carry ice or move tables or something. Over the years, Marcie Gras has blossomed into the event that it is today.

From the outset of this cookbook project, Marcie knew that I would include the story of Marcie Gras. I remember the shock that appeared on my petite wife's face when she learned that the story of her birthday party would wind up in the section of cookbook normally reserved for recipes that include more calories than she would eat in a week and more sour cream than she would eat in a lifetime.

In my mind I can hear her asking, "Can't you just put the Marcie Gras story with the small plate recipes?"

My mental reply is always the same. "How can I make Paella for fifty sound like a small plate?"

Marcie Gras Paella

Chicken and yellow rice was a special treat at Grandmaw Allen's house. If only I had known as a child that it would have been even better by adding sausage and seafood! All of the work for this dish is in the prep work. It's well worth the time as the finished result is always a hit. The combination of chicken, sausage, seafood, and rice means that there's something for everyone. I've made this recipe with Andouille sausage and experimented with lobster, clams, and crab in the dish as well. Feel free to add them as they only serve to enhance to flavor of the dish even further. I've scaled down the recipe to 8 (very hearty) servings so you can imagine the ingredient list for the version that serves fifty!

For Turnin' and Burnin'

12" Saucepan
2 Large Bowls
Chef's Knife
Cutting Board
Measuring Spoon
Measuring Cup
Baking Dish
Bottle Opener

Ingredients

5 tbsp. olive oil
6 Italian sausages, sliced crosswise into 1 inch pieces
4 boneless, skinless chicken breasts cut into 1 inch chunks
1 lb. medium shrimp, peeled and deveined
2 dozen medium mussels or clams, thoroughly washed
2 cups yellow rice
2 tbsp. saffron
32 oz low sodium chicken broth
1 cup green peas
10 garlic cloves, minced
4 onions, roughly chopped
3 tbsp. Black Pepper
2 tbsp. Salt

To Swill while you Grill

You'll be spending quite a bit of time in a hot kitchen to prepare the Paella. Lots of chopping. Lot's of cooking. Drink beer while you cook and save the Rioja and Sauvignon Blanc for the dinner table. After all those beers, you'll be ready to relax with a glass of wine.

Preparation

- Preheat the oven to 350 degrees.
- On the stovetop, over medium high heat in a large saucepan, sauté the chicken in 2 Tbsp of the olive oil for about 5 or until nicely browned.
- Spoon the chicken into a large bowl and set aside.
- Add 1 Tbsp of olive oil, half of the garlic and the sausages to the saucepan and brown the sausages with the garlic for 8 minutes.
- Add to the bowl with the chicken.
- Add one more tbsp of olive oil and the onions to the saucepan.
- Sautee the onions until translucent, about 5 minutes.
- Set aside in a separate bowl.

- Using the remaining Tbsp. of the olive oil, sauté the shrimp for about 4 minutes and add to the chicken and sausage mixture.
- In a large, 3 inch deep baking dish, add the rice, chicken broth, and peas.
- Stir in the saffron.
- Add the onions, sausage, chicken, shrimp, salt and pepper and stir until well mixed.
- Cook for 1 hour or until the rice becomes tender and the chicken and sausage are cooked throughout.
- Remove from oven and stir mixture to fluff the rice.
- Add the mussels or clams evenly over the top of the dish and return to oven for 10 minutes or until the shells open.
- Remove from oven and stir the casserole to evenly distribute the shellfish with the rest of the dish.
- Serve hot.

Mac and Cheese and Cheese and Cheese

Ah, the artery clogging power of cheese or, as I like to call it, "Nature's Perfect Food". (I also call vodka "Vitamin V," so keep in mind that my euphemisms should be taken with a grain of salt.) There are two warnings that you need to be aware of before preparing this recipe. First, your kids may never want to go back to the boxed version of "mac and cheese" after eating this. Second, and perhaps even more important, under no circumstances should you serve this dish on the day before Grandpa has his cholesterol screening.

Otherwise, have at it. Prepare as is for a side dish or mix in cooked Italian sausage or cubes of ham to create a main course casserole.

For Turnin' and Burnin'
2 Medium Sauté Pans
Small Saucepot
Chef's Knife
Cutting Board
Mixing Bowl
Measuring Spoon
Baking Dish
Corkscrew
Wine Glass

Ingredients
16 oz. macaroni (elbows, shells, or other hollowed macaroni)
16 oz. Cheese Whiz
32 oz. Velveeta cheese, sliced into 1 inch pieces
16 oz. shredded sharp cheddar cheese
8 oz. milk
2 tbsp. thyme, minced
4 oz. butter, softened
1 tbsp. olive oil
2 tsp. kosher salt
1 tsp. black pepper

To Swill while you Grill

Okay, so the Italian comes out a little whenever I cook pasta, regardless of its final form. I like to open a nice bottle of red wine, maybe an Amarone or Super Tuscan, and have it with the mac and cheese as a meal unto itself. If serving with a protein, I recommend deferring to the wine best paired with that protein.

Preparation

- Make sure your portable heart defibrillator is charged up and ready to go.
- Preheat oven to 375 degrees.
- Bring 3 quarts of water to a boil in a 6-quart stockpot.
- Add one tsp. of olive oil and the salt.
- Add the macaroni and cook on high temperature for 6 – 8 minutes, depending on the type of macaroni chosen or until the macaroni is tender.
- Pour the macaroni into a colander and shake to strain off the water.
- Transfer the pasta to a casserole dish and mix with the cheese whiz.
- Arrange the Velveeta evenly throughout the casserole.
- Add the milk, thyme, remaining salt, and pepper.
- Bake for 30 minutes.
- Remove from oven.
- Add the milk, stir the mixture, and return to oven. Cook for an additional 20 minutes or until the casserole has absorbed all of the milk.
- Remove from the oven once more and top with the sharp cheddar.
- Return to the oven for 10 more minutes to melt the cheddar.
- Precut casseroles into 3-inch squares and serve.

Undeniably Italian

Throughout this collection of stories and recipes, it's probably fairly easy to see the Italian influence in my cooking. If that point had not already been obvious to you, please refer to the section of chicken recipes that I've included. My mother is half Sicilian. I grew up thinking that green beans tasted awfully plain unless they were cooked with fresh garlic (or at the very least sprinkled with garlic powder).

We ate some form of pasta at least two or three times a week growing up in my Mom's house. By the time I was in first grade, I was certain that garlic, oregano, pasta, and meat sauce were the four basic food groups. (I later learned that the correct food group categories are butter, sugar, grits, and beer).

My siblings are almost as accomplished at eating Italian food as I am. It's not for a lack of effort on their part that they haven't yet surpassed me in this area. They would be more accomplished at eating Italian food than I except that I'm older than they are and have had more practice. They are also very discerning in their tastes. Rest assured that I would not dream of serving any of them an Italian dish that I had not:

a) Tested and refined until I knew it would pass the Pete, Alica, and Sandy test, and

b) Made in quantity sufficient to feed a small army

To come up short on the former might cause me years of ridicule within the family, and to underestimate the latter might just start a riot at the dining table.

Red Headed Red Sauce

I'm the redhead in the family. My brothers, like my mom, are dark haired and olive skinned. My sister is a brunette. My dad, before he became "follicly challenged" was dark haired. I always thought it was odd that the milkman and I were the only two red-haired people that I knew. Kidding aside, I always felt like I was somehow "less Italian" than my siblings because of my hair color – not because of anything they ever said, just my own childhood insecurities - and my red sauce would somehow make me as Italian as they were.

For this reason, I have been developing this sauce for longer than I can remember and have probably served this sauce to more guests than anything else that I make. In fact, this is the first dish that I taught my boys to cook. To this day, if you were to ask them, "If you're making red sauce, what do you need to be doing if you aren't doing anything?" they would reply at once "Add garlic!"

This sauce takes a lot of time, care, and stirring. The last thing you want is to have a sauce that you've been cultivating for several hours to stick to the bottom of the saucepot and burn. The ingredient list includes ½ a cup of red wine for the sauce. You'll enjoy having the remainder of the bottle to keep you company as you stir and adjust flavors as your sauce matures over the hours.

The unusual thing about the sauce is, of course, that there are potatoes in the recipe. Most people like the potatoes, a few don't.

Jordan, my youngest son, isn't a fan of the potatoes. No big smell, Jordy just makes sure not to ladle potatoes onto his pasta as part of his sauce.

Keep them in, make French fries with them; either way, you won't offend me. Potatoes aren't the star of this dish; rather, the interactions of the tomatoes, proteins, herbs, and vegetables with each other and with the miracle of time make this the ultimate comfort food that I will always come back to. That plus the memories.

For Turnin' and Burnin'
Large Stockpot
Measuring Spoon
Large Sauté Pan
Chef's Knife
Cutting Board
Mixing Bowl
Slotted Spoon
Baking Dish
Corkscrew
Wine Glass

Ingredients
3 quarts tomatoes, roasted, peeled, and pulsed in a food processor until chopped
1 ½ lbs. lean ground sirloin
2 lbs. mild Italian sausage, cut into 2 inch portions
3 large potatoes, peeled and cut into 1 inch cubes
2 onions, sliced in half, then sliced crosswise
8 oz. sliced mushrooms
10 cloves garlic, peeled and minced
4 tbsp. olive oil
½ cup dry red wine (like Chianti) for the sauce
Remainder of bottle of red wine (for the chef)
3 tbsp. dried oregano
2 tbsp. dried basil
2 bay leaves
8 oz. shredded mozzarella cheese
Garlic powder
Kosher salt
Black pepper

To Swill while you Grill
When the boys were little, I drank Chianti from a coffee cup while standing over the sauce and stirring it for hours. I've progressed to a wine glass but still like a Chianti Classico with my red sauce. I suppose that eventually, I'll cut out the middleman and drink straight from the bottle.

Preparation
- In a large stockpot, over medium high heat, add the tomatoes, potatoes, onions, mushrooms, minced garlic, bay leaves and one tbsp of the olive oil.
- Add 1 tablespoon each of garlic powder, oregano, and basil, and a teaspoon each of salt and black pepper to the sauce.
- Cook, for 20 minutes, stirring often.

- After 20 minutes reduce heat to simmer.
- As your base sauce is cooking, sauté the ground sirloin in salt pepper and a little garlic powder, pinching off pieces of ground sirloin as you add it to the pan instead of crumbling as you might for chili. Add the beef to the base sauce.
- Using a slotted spoon to drain off some of the juices could help to delay the onset of a negative cardiac event.
- After cooking the beef, cook the sausage in the same manner, with garlic, salt, and pepper, turning often until well browned.
- Add sausage to the sauce and stir well.
- Add the red wine to the sauce, the remaining olive oil, oregano and basil.
- Stir in the mozzarella.
- Adjust to taste with Garlic powder, salt and pepper.
- Stir often, continuing to simmer. The longer you have to cook this dish, the better, as the flavors of the various ingredients will interact with each other to bring a progressively subtle flavor to the sauce.
- Serve this over pasta toped with grated parmesan or Asiago or spoon onto a sub roll and melt provolone on top for a tasty sandwich. Separating the liquid gives a great base for veal of chicken Parmesan. The liquid and beef together provide your sauce component for lasagna.

Sausage and Ricotta Stuffed Manicotti

Manicotti, which always sounded like, "manna-GOAT" when my grandfather pronounced it, was a treat for special occasions. I like to think of manicotti as an Italian burrito. You can stuff a burrito with a variety of fillings and it's still a burrito. The same is true of manicotti. I use my Red Headed Red Sauce as the sauce component for the dish and top with grated Asiago cheese.

For Turnin' and Burnin'
2-quart Saucepot
Large Saucepan
Measuring Spoon
Measuring Cup
Chef's Knife
Cutting Board
Mixing Bowl
Baking Dish
Corkscrew
Wine Glass

Ingredients
2 cups liquid from Red Headed Red Sauce or other red pasta sauce
14 uncooked manicotti shells

Bill Allen

1 lb. ground Italian sausage, (hot or mild)
15 oz. Ricotta cheese
1 tbsp. garlic powder
½ cup onion, diced
4 tbsp. olive oil
¼ cup dry red wine (like Chianti) for the sauce
2 glasses of red wine (for the chef)
1 tsp. dried oregano
1 tsp. dried basil
8 oz. shredded mozzarella cheese

To Swill while you Grill

Normally, I'll make a dent in our Italian-Red stash while stuffing the pasta tubes, then more of one while baking them. A quarter cup of wine goes in the recipe, a glass of wine goes in the chef. Repeat for the chef as often as necessary.

Preparation

- In a 2-quart saucepot, bring the red sauce to a simmer.
- In a large saucepan, over medium-high heat, heat the olive oil.
- Add the onions ¼ cup of red wine and sauté for 2 minutes.
- Add the sausage and cook until browned or about 8 minutes.
- Remove the sausage and onion mixture, drain off the liquid, transfer sausage and onions to a large mixing bowl, and allow to cool.
- Preheat oven to 350 degrees.
- Once the sausage mixture has cooled, stir in the ricotta, oregano, and basil.
- Stuff the resulting mixture into the uncooked manicotti shells.
- Place stuffed shells cooking into a lightly oiled, 2 inch deep, 9" x 13" baking dish over a thin coating of sauce to help prevent the shells from sticking during and cover with more of the red sauce.
- Cook for 1 hour.
- Baste with additional red sauce at 30 minutes, making sure to cover the pasta shells. (If you can see the top of the manicotti, it likely needs a little extra sauce to keep it from drying out.)
- This is a good time to drink those 2 glasses of wine as your house fills with the incomparable aroma of pasta, sausage, and red sauce cooking.
- Once an hour has passed, remove the baking dish from the oven and evenly sprinkle the mozzarella cheese on top.
- Return the manicotti to the oven and cook for an additional 5 minutes or until the cheese is melted.
- Ladle red sauce onto each plate, then place 2 of the manicotti shells over the red sauce per plate.
- Serve with Italian Garlic Bread and pair with a glass of Sangiovese.

Crispy Eggplant Parmesan

I usually to shy away from eggplant in restaurants because it tends to arrive at the table as a soggy nebulous goo, swimming in red sauce and suffocated by cheese. It's a shame, too, since crispy eggplant slices are a favorite option for my twice a year foray into the world of a meatless meal.

For Turnin' and Burnin'
Kitchen Tongs
Large Saucepan
Measuring Spoon
Chef's Knife
Cutting Board
Mixing Bowl
Baking Dish
Corkscrew
Wine Glass

Ingredients
2 cups liquid from Red Headed Red Sauce or other red pasta sauce
3 eggplant, peeled and sliced crosswise into ¼ inch discs
1 cup Italian flavored breadcrumbs
2 eggs, beaten
1 cup Parmesan cheese, shredded
4 tbsp. olive oil
Salt
Pepper

To Swill while you Grill
To me, nothing smells more like an Italian kitchen than eggplant browning in olive oil. Savor this aroma while enjoying a glass of Sangiovese.

Preparation
- Preheat oven to 350 degrees.
- Evenly spread the sauce into a 9" x 13" x 2" baking dish.
- Dip each of the eggplant discs into the egg wash, then lightly coat in the breadcrumbs.
- In a large saucepan, over medium-high heat, heat the olive oil.
- Brown the eggplant in the olive oil until crispy, about 2 minutes per side.
- Transfer the eggplant to the baking dish, setting each disc on top of the sauce.
- Top the eggplant with grated Parmesan cheese.
- Bake for 5 minutes or until sauce is hot and cheese is melted.
- Serve with Italian Garlic Bread and an additional glass of Sangiovese.

Sausage Stuffed Hot Peppers
If left to my own devices, I would have a small portion of Sausage Stuffed Hot Peppers as an appetizer every day and a large portion as a meal every other day. The heat of the sausage competes

with the heat of the peppers for attention in this recipe; yet, the sauce and cheese bring an acidity and richness that makes this more than just another spicy entrée.

For Turnin' and Burnin'
Rubber Spatula
Large Saucepan
Measuring Spoon
Chef's Knife
Cutting Board
Mixing Bowl
Large Baking Dish
Corkscrew
Wine Glass

Ingredients
2 cups liquid from Red Headed Red Sauce or other red pasta sauce
8 Anaheim peppers, halved lengthwise and seeded
1¼ lbs. ground hot Italian sausage, casings removed if present
½ cup mozzarella cheese, shredded
¼ cup Italian flavored breadcrumbs
1 egg, beaten
1 cup Parmesan cheese, finely grated
2 tbsp. olive oil
1 tsp. powdered garlic
1 tsp. dried oregano
1 tsp. dried basil
½ tsp. salt
½ tsp. freshly ground black pepper

To Swill while you Grill
I suppose that I could recommend Sangiovese for any of my recipes that include red sauce, but in this case I won't. Personally, I'd drink a preemptive beer while preparing the stuffed peppers. They are going to be really hot.

Preparation
- Preheat oven to 350 degrees.
- In a saucepot, bring red sauce to a simmer, stirring often.
- In a large saucepan over medium heat, add the sausage and cook until thoroughly browned, about 8 minutes.
- Remove sausage from heat, drain off and discard drippings, and transfer sausage to a large mixing bowl and let cool.
- Add mozzarella cheese, breadcrumbs, egg, olive oil, garlic, oregano, basil, salt, and pepper to the mixing bowl. Mix by hand until all ingredients are well combined.
- Place the pepper halves into the baking dish and stuff each pepper with the sausage mixture.

- Cook in the oven for 20 minutes.
- Remove from the oven to top the stuffed peppers with parmesan cheese. Return to oven and cook 5 minutes more or until cheese is melted.
- Plate the peppers over ladled red sauce. Grate additional Parmesan cheese in a side dish if desired.
- Serve with Italian Garlic Bread and an additional glass of Sangiovese.

Italian Rosemary Garlic Bread

Instead of burning your mouth when taste testing my (now your) red sauce recipe, why not spoon the sauce onto a nice piece of homemade Italian bread for tasting? A word of caution though - if you follow the directions for this bread precisely as well as the one for Red Headed Red Sauce, you will have consumed at least 5 glasses of wine during the preparation of the two recipes. Hopefully, you're cooking at home and won't need to drive at the end of the evening! Serve this with any Italian entrée or along side Italian meats and cheeses as a hearty starter.

For Turnin' and Burnin'
Cutting Board
Measuring Spoon
Measuring Cup
Sifter
Mixing Bowl
Damp Cloth
Cookie Sheet
Corkscrew
Wine glass

Ingredients
3 cups all-purpose flour
1 packet of active dry yeast
1 cup water
1 tsp. salt
3 sprigs rosemary, minced
1 tbsp. garlic powder
2 tbsp. olive oil
2 glasses of Barbera or other red wine

To Swill while you Grill
To properly follow the Rubaiyat (of Omar Khayyam) line, I guess a jug of wine and a "thou" would be the perfect swilling companions. If you're cooking alone, try a glass or two of Barbera.

Preparation
- Take off your rings and bracelets and put them in a safe place.
- Sift the flour, garlic powder and salt into a large mixing bowl.
- Create a crater in the center of the bowl.

- Add the yeast and pour the water on top of the yeast. Wait for about 5 to 6 minutes until the yeast begins to bubble.
- Pour yourself a glass of wine during the waiting period and let it breathe. (*Wait, don't drink it yet!*)
- Add the rosemary.
- Mix the flour, rosemary, and water in the mixing bowl until you have a something that resembles a big firm dough ball more than it does glue, meaning, of course, that the dough is no longer sticky. (Add additional flour if necessary to aid in this process.)
- Remove dough from mixing bowl and place on a floured cutting board or countertop.
- Knead the dough for 5 to 10 minutes.
- Place the dough into a floured bowl and cover with a damp cloth, like Marcie's grandmother used to do, and let rest in a warm place (80 – 85 degrees) for about one hour and a half or until the dough rises and doubles in size.
- Now is the perfect time to drink that glass of wine that you poured earlier.
- Preheat oven to 400 degrees.
- Return the dough to the countertop or cutting board and give it a few good whacks with the palms of your hands.
- Please the dough onto a cookie sheet that is coated in cornmeal.
- Reform the dough into a loaf and brush olive oil over the top of the loaf.
- Sprinkle sesame seeds over the top of the loaf and bake for 45 minutes.
- Adjust cooking time based on how brown you like for your bread to be cooked.
- Wash your hands and put your rings and bracelets back on before you forget and they get lost.
- While the bread is cooking, go ahead – have that second glass of wine.
- Slice bread and serve hot with butter.

Sauces, Marinades, Dressings, and Rubs

I have always looked at dining in a restaurant as "an event". First you have to decide what type of food you'd like to eat and where you'd like to go. (If more than two people are involved, simply deciding where to go can turn into a debate of congressional proportion). Then there's the challenge of making reservations. If you're fortunate, you'll be able to get a table at the restaurant you want at the time you'd like, on the date you'd like; if not, you'll need to repeat this process until you meet with success. You'll probably want to dress a little bit better than for dinner alone at home (read: this may be the chance you've been looking for to buy those fabulous new shoes). But I digress.

To me, the things that set dining out apart from eating at home more than anything else are appetizers, presentation, and finishing touches like sauces. Well, that, and (hopefully) a very nice person treating you like a guest in their home that brings you whatever you would like to drink as often as you'd like, brings you your dinner, cleans up the mess and thanks you for coming to see them and asks you to come back anytime you'd like. You leave with a spring in your step that is part joy and part due to the fact that the weight of your wallet has been (sometimes) significantly reduced.

Look at the descriptions of various main dishes on a restaurant menu sometime. You're likely to see the protein described in flourishing terms, ones that use more adjectives than should be allowed by law. That and how the dish is finished. The sauce or topping.

Assuming you have a grill, you can grill a pork chop with some salt and pepper at home. You can serve it on a plate with a vegetable and a starch and have a perfectly fine dinner. It only takes a small amount of effort to take that same dinner to the next level. A quick spice rub for the pork before cooking and an easy mango salsa topping will elevate that plain grilled pork chop to what I like to call "restaurant quality". A black peppercorn and red wine reduction with a piece of grilled beef will have the same effect. Get the idea? Sauces and finishing touches can transform a dish from ordinary to "wow!"

Salsa Verde (Green Chili Sauce)

Salsa Verde gets its color from the green tomatoes (tomatillos) used in its preparation. By varying the type and number of peppers used, and the length of cooking time, you can control the spicy heat of this sauce. The longer you cook, the milder it becomes. This salsa is quite versatile. Try it with tortilla chips as an easy appetizer. Use it on tacos or breakfast Shrimpanadas. In addition to being a natural match for Mexican dishes, this green sauce is a winner with roasted pork tenderloin and lamb.

For Turnin' and Burnin'
Cutting Board
Measuring Spoon
Measuring Cup
Chef's Knife
Food Processor
Saucepot
Serving Bowl

Ingredients

2 tbsp. olive oil
12 medium tomatillos, (outer husk removed) washed and chopped
Juice of 1 lime
2 cloves garlic, chopped
3 Serrano chiles, chopped
1 medium onion, chopped
1 ½ tsp. kosher salt
1 tsp. black pepper
3 tbsp. chopped cilantro

Preparation

- Combine the olive oil, tomatillos, garlic, and lime juice in a food processor and pulse until well mixed and finely chopped.
- Transfer to a 2 quart saucepot; add chiles, onion, cilantro, salt, and pepper.
- Bring to a boil for and cook for 10 minutes.
- Reduce heat to simmer and cook for 30 minutes more.
- Remove from heat, transfer to a bowl. The salsa may be served hot (as a sauce for roast tenderloin or lamb) or at room temperature as a condiment for Mexican dishes.

Roasted Tomato Salsa Roja (Red Chili Sauce)

The differences between my salsa roja and my salsa verde are quite straightforward. I use red tomatoes instead of tomatillos in the salsa roja and roast and core the tomatoes before combining them with the other ingredients. I'll normally use chipotle peppers to make this salsa very spicy and serve it on the side with any of my recipes that call for Pico de Gallo.

For Turnin' and Burnin'

Cutting Board
Measuring Spoon
Measuring Cup
Chef's Knife
Baking Dish
Saucepot
Food Processor
Serving Bowl

Ingredients

1 tbsp. olive oil
8 Roma tomatoes, washed
Juice of 1 lime
3 Chipotle peppers in adobo sauce
¾ cup cilantro, chopped
1 ½ tsp. ground cumin

1 tsp. kosher salt
1 tsp. black pepper

Preparation
- Preheat broiler.
- Coat Baking dish with 1 tbsp of olive oil.
- Place tomatoes on baking dish and broil until tomatoes are slightly charred, about 8 minutes.
- Remove tomatoes from oven; allow to cool, and then core and chop the tomatoes.
- Add chopped tomatoes, chipotles, cilantro, lime juice, and cumin to a food processor and pulse until well mixed and finely chopped.
- Remove from heat, transfer to a bowl to serve.

Cabernet and Black Peppercorn Reduction

A cabernet and black peppercorn reduction provides a simple yet amazing finishing touch to beef, especially filet mignon.

For Turnin' and Burnin'
Saucepan
Cutting Board
Chef's Knife
Measuring Spoon
Measuring Cup

Ingredients
¼ cup beef stock
½ cup Cabernet Sauvignon
1 tbsp. black peppercorns
2 oz butter
2 spring onions, diced
½ tsp. kosher salt
1 tsp. black pepper

Preparation
- Bring the stock and the wine to a boil in a saucepan.
- Add the peppercorns and onion and reduce heat to simmer.
- Reduce by half.
- Add the butter and stir until butter is melted.
- Adjust flavor with salt and pepper to taste.
- Serve over beef.

Raspberry and Red Zin Reduction

This reduction was debuted at the cookout that I described when introducing my pork recipes. The sweetness of this reduction is a nice change of pace from the usual savory sauces that you might find served with beef. Sliced beef tenderloin is a good match for the raspberries, thyme, and zinfandel.

For Turnin' and Burnin'

Saucepan
Cutting Board
Blender
Chef's Knife
Measuring Spoon
Measuring Cup

Ingredients

1½ cups fresh raspberries
½ cup (red) Zinfandel
2 tbsp. sugar
2 oz. butter
3 tbsp. fresh thyme
½ tsp. kosher salt
1 tsp. black pepper

Preparation

- Over medium high heat on the stovetop, add the wine, butter, and thyme to a medium saucepan. Bring to a boil, and then reduce heat to simmer.
- Puree raspberries in a blender; then pour the puree through a strainer into the saucepan.
- Stir in the sugar, salt, and pepper and continue to cook until reduced by half or about 3 minutes. Cooking too long will result in less sweetness.
- Serve over beef tenderloin.

Tangy Southern Barbeque Sauce

This barbeque sauce will take you less than five minutes to make. I use this sauce on ribs, in my Barbequed Cole Slaw, added to marinades, and as a topping for grilled pork tenderloin.

For Turnin' and Burnin'

Measuring Spoon
Measuring Cup
Mixing Bowl

Ingredients

4 oz. catsup
2 oz. yellow mustard
2 oz. A1 Steak Sauce
1 tsp. fresh ground horseradish
1 tsp. honey
1 tsp. hot sauce (like Tabasco)
Ground black pepper

Preparation

- Combine all ingredients in a mixing bowl and stir well.
- Keeps refrigerated for 1 week. Makes 1 cup.

Argentine Chimichurri

"Chimi" is as essential to the Argentine dinner table as Pico de Gallo is to its Mexican counterpart. Based on a combination of parsley, garlic, olive oil, and vinegar, this sauce is equally at home on empanadas, beef dishes, Provoletta, and even as a dipping sauce for bread. It's quick and easy to make to boot.

For Turnin' and Burnin'

Cutting Board
Measuring Spoon
Measuring Cup
Chef's Knife
Mixing Bowl

Ingredients

1 cup olive oil
¼ cup malt vinegar
1 cup fresh parsley, diced
3 – 4 cloves of garlic, depending on size of cloves
1 medium onion, finely minced
1 tsp. ground black pepper
1 tsp. kosher salt
1 tsp. dried oregano
1 tsp. red pepper flakes
Dash of paprika

Preparation

- Combine all of the dry ingredients in a mixing bowl.
- Toss in the diced parsley and vinegar and mix well.
- Wait a few minutes for the parley and (formerly) dry ingredients to marinate in the vinegar. 5 to 10 minutes should be sufficient.
- Add the oil and mix all ingredients well.
- Keeps refrigerated for 5 days if covered in an airtight container. Makes 1 cup.

Prime Rib Marinade

Prime Rib is a marriage of beautiful beef and a tasty crust. This combination of herbs and olive oil will produce a crisp crust that is a wonderful compliment to the tenderness of roasted beef.

For Turnin' and Burnin'
Cutting Board
Measuring Spoon
Measuring Cup
Chef's Knife
Mixing Bowl

Ingredients
8 cloves of garlic, finely minced
6 tbsp. fresh rosemary, chopped
3 tbsp. fresh thyme, chopped
3 tbsp. dried oregano
6 tbsp. coarsely ground black pepper
1 tsp. salt
1 cup olive oil

Preparation
- Combine all of the dry ingredients in a mixing bowl.
- Add the oil and mix all ingredients well.
- Use to marinate standing rib roast 2 hours prior to cooking.

Zin-Rosemary Lamb Marinade

This marinade leverages the fruit forward presence of the Zin with rosemary to create a nice richness that will stand up to a grilled rack of lamb.

Ingredients
¼ cup olive oil
3 tbsp. balsamic vinegar
3 cloves garlic, minced
1 tsp. kosher salt
1 tsp. freshly ground black pepper
4 tbsp. rosemary, minced
1 cup red Zinfandel wine

Preparation
- Combine all ingredients in a large mixing bowl and thoroughly combine.
- Use to marinate racks of lamb or individual chops 2 hours prior to cooking.

Horseradish Cream Sauce

This is one of those little "extra effort steps" that can set your dinner apart. Instead of buying a creamed horseradish sauce from the market, take five minutes and whip this one up. You (and your guests) will be glad that you did.

For Turnin' and Burnin'
Measuring Spoon
Measuring Cup
Wire Whisk
Large Bowl

Ingredients
2 cups sour cream
½ cup prepared horseradish
Juice of 1 lemon
1 tsp. salt

Preparation
- Combine all ingredients in a mixing bowl and whisk vigorously until sauce is creamy.
- Serve with beef.

Classic Hollandaise Sauce

Hollandaise sauce, one of the five "Mother Sauces" in French cooking (along with Béchamel sauce, Espagnole sauce, Tomato sauce, and Velouté sauce) is a base sauce from which other sauces can be built. The trick in getting this sauce right is making sure that you don't get the eggs so hot that they will scramble. This sauce makes a beautiful topping for everything from Eggs Benedict (see Benedict Allen recipe) to grilled asparagus. It will also serve as the base recipe for the Béarnaise sauce recipe that follows in this section.

For Turnin' and Burnin'
Measuring Spoon
Measuring Cup
Wire Whisk
Large Bowl
Large Saucepan

Ingredients
2 egg yolks
1 (4 oz.) stick of butter, melted
1 tsp. lemon juice
1 tsp. salt
Pinch cayenne pepper

Preparation
- Heat 1 cup of water in a saucepan over medium heat until simmering but not boiling.
- In a heat resistant bowl, whisk toe egg yolks and lemon juice. Holding toe bowl over the heat but not allowing it to touch the water, slowly whisk in the melted butter.
- Continue whisking until sauce thickens.
- Remove from heat and whisk in the salt and cayenne pepper.
- Serve warm.

Quick and Easy Béarnaise Sauce

Béarnaise sauce is a wonderful complement to grilled beef, especially beef prepared "Oscar" style (topped with crab meat). For this sauce, I'm assuming that you have done your homework and reviewed the recipe for Hollandaise sauce on the previous page. Using the finished hollandaise as your base, it's a simple matter to make a quick Béarnaise. A more classical method would call for the omission of the lemon juice from the recipe, and you are welcome to leave it out, but if you're in a hurry, the little bit of lemon juice won't hurt.

For Turnin' and Burnin'
Measuring Spoon
Measuring Cup
Wire Whisk
Large Bowl
Large Saucepan

Ingredients
½ cup Classic Hollandaise Sauce
2 tbsp. dry white wine
1 tbsp. finely chopped shallots or spring onion
1 tsp. dried tarragon

Preparation
- Assuming your completed hollandaise sauce is still in the large bowl that we used in the previous recipe; transfer it to a saucepan over low heat.
- Immediately whisk in shallots, wine, and tarragon. Add a tablespoon of water if necessary to thin the sauce.
- Remove from heat.
- Drizzle over beef or seafood and serve immediately.

Toasted Garlic and Blue Cheese Crème Sauce

Serve this as a topping for beef tenderloin or serve on the side with roasted beef. The toasted garlic adds a nice twist.

For Turnin' and Burnin'
Saucepan
Cutting Board
Measuring Spoon
Measuring Cup
Spoon
Chef's Knife
Mixing Bowl

Ingredients
¾ cup heavy cream
1 garlic clove, finely minced
5 oz. bleu cheese crumbles
1 tbsp. freshly cracked black pepper

Preparation
- Toast the garlic in a saucepan over medium heat until golden, taking care not to burn.
- Heat the cream to a boil, then reduce and simmer for 8 to 10 minutes or until the cream coats the back of a spoon.
- Remove from the heat and transfer to a mixing bowl.
- Add the bleu cheese, garlic, and black pepper and mix well.

Honey Poppy Seed Dressing

The contrast of pepper and sweetness in this dressing make it a favorite among our crowd of friends. Serve it over Strawberry Bleu Salad, Cheese and Greens and Fruit, Oh My! or use it as a baste for grilled chicken breasts.

For Turnin' and Burnin'
Measuring Cup
Measuring Spoons
Wire Whisk
Salad Dressing Cruet

Ingredients
2/3 cup canola oil
4 tbsp. honey
3 tbsp. lemon juice
2 tbsp. poppy seeds
¾ tbsp. ground mustard
½ tsp. salt
½ tsp. black pepper

Bill Allen

<u>*Preparation*</u>
- Add oil to measuring cup, and then add other ingredients.
- Whisk all ingredients together until thoroughly combined.
- Transfer to dressing cruet.
- Shake well before serving.

Vegetables, Salads, and Sides

Remember when you were growing up? How many times did your parents say to you, "Eat your vegetables"? In our house it was more like, "Bill, don't eat all the vegetables, save some for the rest of us!" With apologies to the boiled okra crowd, I like almost all vegetables. That being said, the title of this book probably gave you an idea that you were not signing up for a primer on vegetarian cooking. I'm including some favorites but don't intend for this to be an exhaustive list of all of the vegetable recipes that I enjoy.

During my childhood, Mom and Grandmaw Allen were regular visitors to the U-Pick fields around Homestead. Occasionally, my siblings and I got to accompany them into the field to pick tomatoes or pole beans. When we returned home, I watched the Mom and Grandmaw can the vegetables that they picked so that we could have fresh tasting vegetables year round.

This was cool, but even better was helping Maw in her garden. I'm not sure that I was actually any "help" to her, but it was fun nonetheless. She grew tomatoes, eggplant, pole beans, radishes, onions, potatoes, carrots, and little hot red peppers (which I later learned were Jamaican Bird Peppers. She always started from seeds, never from plants. We'd plant, wait seemingly forever for the new plants to break ground, water them, weed them, and watch them grow. Finally, when we harvested from Maw's garden and enjoyed the fresh vegetables that she had grown, there was a special joy in having been part of the seed-to-plate process that had taken place.

As with casseroles, plan to pair vegetables and other sides with wine based on the protein that is being served. If having the vegetables or sides without a protein, drink champagne to celebrate a meatless meal.

Grilled Mixed Vegetable Medley

You can do this dish perfectly well in the oven but I find that maneuvering this dish is easier if done on the grill. Use your favorite fresh vegetables in this one but be sure to include the tomatoes and onions. The emulsification of the tomatoes and the ability of the onion flavor and aroma to permeate the other vegetables are what give this dish its distinctive flavor. I've used corn and potatoes in this dish as well; it just depends on the crowd. To make this dish spicy, add a couple of halved jalapenos or serranos.

For Turnin' and Burnin'
Mr. Grill
Aluminum Foil
Measuring Spoon
Cutting Board
Chef's Knife
Mixing Bowl

Ingredients

1 zucchini squash, cut into ½ inch by 2 inch sticks
1 yellow squash, cut into ½ inch by 2 inch sticks
2 carrots cut into ½ inch by 2 inch sticks
2 tomatoes, quartered
2 onions cut into wedges
4 oz. Sliced mushrooms
4 garlic cloves, peeled and whole
2 jalapeño chiles, sliced in half, seeds removed (optional)
4 tbsp. olive oil
3 sprigs of rosemary, whole
1 tbsp. fresh thyme
1 ½ tsp. kosher salt
1 tsp. black pepper

Preparation

- Combine all of the vegetables and the garlic cloves in a large bowl.
- Add the olive oil and stir, making sure that all of the vegetables are coated.
- Add the thyme, rosemary, salt and pepper and stir to mix.
- Transfer the vegetable mixture to a sheet of aluminum foil. The foil sheet should be large enough that when the four corners are pulled up, they can easily meet and cover the vegetables.
- Flip the covered vegetables over onto a second sheet of foil and repeat the process. This will prevent steam and juices from escaping when cooking.
- On a hot grill, cook for 20 minutes, turn, and cook for an additional 20 minutes or until vegetables are cooked to desired texture.
- Unwrap foil, transfer to a large serving bowl, discarding the rosemary stems and excess juice.

Strawberry Bleu Salad

This salad may be the easiest recipe that you'll ever find, short of opening a bag of chips. The sweetness of fresh strawberries paired with the tanginess of bleu cheese and topped with Honey Poppy Seed dressing will add color and flavor to your lunch plate.

For Turnin' and Burnin'

Measuring Spoon
Cutting Board
Cheese Grater
Chef's Knife

Ingredients

4 strawberries, capped, washed, and sliced thinly
2 tbsp. bleu cheese, grated
2 tbsp. Honey Poppy Seed Dressing

- Arrange the strawberries on a chilled plate.
- Grate the bleu cheese over the strawberries.
- Top with Honey Poppy Seed dressing.

Cheese and Greens and Fruit, Oh My!

Let's make a salad. Okay, I guess we'll need to narrow that plan down a little. The word "salad" encompasses a broad range of foods. Reminiscent of Bubba in _Forrest Gump_, most of us can think of quite a list of different kinds of salads. Green salad, shrimp salad, jello salad, tuna salad, fruit salad, ham salad, egg salad, taco salad…. (I haven't quite mastered salad kebobs or salad etouffee yet!). You get the point though. Salad can mean almost anything with two or more ingredients, depending on whom you ask. Since we don't have all day to decide, let's approach this logically.

To me, when I think of salad, the first word that comes to mind is lettuce. Interestingly enough, _šalat,_ (pronounced SHAL-aht) is the Slovak word for lettuce. Therefore, out of respect for the eastern European etymological influence on salads, we'll include some different types of lettuce in our salad.

The Spanish words for strawberries and oranges are _fresa_ and _naranja,_ respectively. Fresa sounds kind of like the "fresh" and I like fresh ingredients. I lived with my grandparents in Naranja, Florida; so let's add some strawberries and mandarin oranges to our salad.

We'll add thinly sliced rings of red onion because I have red hair and palm hearts because there is a palm tree outside of my kitchen window. Marcie is half Greek, so we'll toss in some feta as well. Does completing the salad with feta make it a fait accompli?

Let's top our salad with some of the leftover Honey Poppy Seed dressing from the fridge (logical, huh?) and realize that there's no problem that can't be solved with a little bit of logical thought.

For Turnin' and Burnin'
Cutting Board
Chef's Knife
Measuring Cup
Large Serving Bowl

Ingredients
6 oz. bag mixed lettuce and spinach blend
8 strawberries, capped, washed, and sliced thinly
11 oz. can mandarin oranges, drained
¼ cup red onion, thinly sliced and separated into rings
3 palm hearts, sliced thinly and separated into rings, inseparable pieces chopped
4 oz. feta cheese, crumbled
½ cup Honey Poppy Seed Dressing

Preparation
- Add the lettuce mix, onion and palm hearts to the salad, tossing well.
- Arrange oranges and strawberries on top of the salad.
- Sprinkle the feta over the top of the salad
- Serve with Honey Poppy Seed dressing on the side.

Wilted Spinach with Bacon

Quick and easy, this spinach dish partners excellently with lamb. The trick is to not overcook the spinach but just enough so that it is wilted.

For Turnin' and Burnin'
12" Sauté Pan
Rubber Spatula
Cutting Board
Chef's Knife

Ingredients
8 oz, fresh spinach
2 garlic cloves, minced
3 strips bacon
Black pepper, freshly ground

Preparation
- Over medium-high heat, cook the bacon in the sauté pan until crisp.
- Remove from heat.
- Reserving the bacon grease in the pan, place bacon on cutting board and allow to cool.
- Crumble or roughly chop the bacon.
- Reheat the bacon grease and add the spinach, garlic, and bacon.
- Cook for 3 minutes or until spinach is wilted, stirring often. Cover when not stirring and checking the progress of the spinach.
- Add black pepper to taste and serve immediately.

Lima Beans Incognito

Now there's a reason to eat those lima beans that you have had in the freezer or pantry all of this time. Lima Beans Incognito tastes great and you'll have the added benefit of gaining much needed storage space.

You'll want to make these into the consistency of mashed potatoes. The limas pair superbly with lamb.

For Turnin' and Burnin'
Saucepot
Food Processor
Cutting Board
Chef's Knife
Measuring Cup
Food Processor

Ingredients
30 oz. lima beans
2 tbsp. olive oil
1 sprig rosemary
1 garlic clove, peeled
Juice of 1 lime
Kosher salt
1 tsp. ground black pepper

Preparation
- In a saucepot in 4 cups of water, cook the limas with the sprig of rosemary and a dash of salt beans for 20 minutes over medium heat.
- Remove from heat, drain, and discard the rosemary.
- In the food processor, add the limas, lime juice, garlic clove, and black pepper. Gradually add the olive oil as you pulse the lima bean mixture until it is the consistency of mashed potatoes.
- Serve hot.

Lobster Mashed Potatoes
For the ultimate in self-indulgence, lobster mashed potatoes are at the top of my list. Truth be told, I'd be pretty happy to eat these as a meal and skip everything else – except the wine of course!

For Turnin' and Burnin'
Large Saucepot
Large Pot with Steamer Insert
Cutting Board
Chef's Knife
Measuring Cup
Mixing Bowl
Colander
Potato Masher

Bill Allen

Ingredients
1 lb. Lobster
2 tbsp. olive oil
2 lbs. potatoes, peeled, and quartered
4 tbsp. butter cut into 1 tbsp. pieces
Kosher salt
¼ cup Milk
1 tsp. ground black pepper
Salt

Preparation
- Bring the potatoes in 4 cups of water to a boil and cook for 20 minutes.
- While the potatoes are cooking, steam the lobster for 10 minutes in the pot with the steamer insert.
- Remove lobster and insert from heat, reserving ½ cup of liquid.
- Remove the lobster from the insert, let cool, and then remove the claw and tail meat from the shell. Finely chop the lobster and set aside.
- When the potatoes have completed cooking, drain the potatoes and transfer to a mixing bowl. Add the butter, milk, pepper, and ½ of the reserved liquid from the lobster and mash until the potatoes are to the desired texture.
- Gradually stir in the lobster.
- Add salt to taste.
- Serve hot.

Yorkshire Pudding

George Bernard Shaw once said, "The English and Americans are two people separated by a common language". Never has this been more evident than in the naming of foods. Bangers and Mash? Sounds like a grunge band. Spotted Dick? Get a shot of penicillin. Toad in the Hole? You might want to go to the "Feed-n-Seed" store and find out how to get rid of it. Yorkshire Pudding? Sounds like a dessert, but it's not.

Yorkshire pudding is an egg, milk, salt, and flour mixture that is combined with hot beef drippings and cooked in either a baking dish or muffin tins. I prefer to use muffin tins as they yield tall, individual servings of this savory alternative to bread or other starch. Serve this with beef (preferably the beef that you cooked to come up with those beef drippings that you're using to make the Yorkshire pudding).

For Turnin' and Burnin'
2 Large Mixing Bowls
Wire Whisk
Cupcake/Muffin Tins
Rubber Spatula

Ingredients

¾ cup beef drippings
1 cup all purpose flour
4 eggs, room temperature
1 cup milk
¾ tsp. kosher salt

Preparation

- In one mixing bowl, combine the eggs and milk and beat until smooth.
- In a second mixing bowl, combine the flour and the salt.
- Gradually add the flour/salt mixture to the egg/milk mixture and whisk until smooth and creamy.
- Refrigerate for at least 2 hours.
- Preheat oven to 450 degrees.
- Divide the beef drippings equally into muffin tins.
- Heat the beef drippings for 3-5 minutes in the oven.
- Remove the muffin tins from the oven. Be careful, as you don't want a trip to the emergency room after giving yourself 3rd degree burns from spilling hot beef fat on yourself. This would be a terrible holiday buzz-kill. But I digress.
- Give the batter a quick stir and pour on top of the beef drippings.
- Return to the oven for 15 to 20 minutes or until the pastry is dry and puffy.
- Serve immediately.

Sautéed Onions and 'Shrooms

My brother, Sandy, and I were at home one day when I was thirteen and he was seven. We decided to make some burgers on the stovetop but didn't see any lettuce or tomatoes or hamburger buns for that matter anywhere in the kitchen. Determined to act like I knew what I was doing (which of course I didn't). I liberated some mushrooms and onions from the refrigerator that our mom, no doubt, was planning to use to make red sauce later in the week. Rationalizing that it would be okay to appropriate a bit of red wine from behind the bar as long as it was for cooking, we sautéed the onions and mushrooms in olive oil with a little wine and thought we had invented the best thing ever! Every time Sandy reminds me of this early kitchen adventure and how much fun we had, I remember how happy I was that we didn't burn the house down.

For Turnin' and Burnin'

12" Sauté Pan
Rubber Spatula
Cutting Board
Chef's Knife

Bill Allen

Ingredients

2 tbsp. olive oil
1 onion, halved then sliced into thin strips
1 tsp. garlic, minced
4 oz. sliced mushrooms
1 Serrano chile, seeded and diced
¼ cup red or white wine (we used red because that was what was already open)
1 tsp. cracked black pepper

Preparation

- Over medium heat in a saucepan, heat the olive oil until hot.
- Add the onions, mushrooms, and chilis and sauté for 5 minutes or until the onions are soft.
- Add the wine and black pepper and sauté for 1 minute more, mixing all ingredients thoroughly.
- Remove from heat and serve as a side dish or topping over beef, chicken, or pork.

Wine Reference

I hope that you'll find this cross-reference based on my "swilling notes" helpful. It lists, by beverage, each of the recipes with which I've recommended pairing that beverage. It's also a useful way if you have a particular drink in mind but can't decide what to eat. (Priorities, right?) The bottom line here is this: drink what you like. Determine what you like and what you don't and go with it. Above all, have fun!

What To Swill	When you Grill
Amarone	Axis of Chicken Parmesan
	Mac and Cheese and Cheese and Cheese
	Sausage and Ricotta Stuffed Manicotti
Baileys Irish Cream	Italian Breakfast Potatoes
Barbera	Sausage Stuffed Mushrooms
	Prosciutto and Swiss Cheese Stuffed Chicken Breasts
	Axis of Chicken Parmesan
	Sausage and Ricotta Stuffed Manicotti
	Italian Rosemary Garlic Bread
Beer	Spicy Shrimp Bisque
	Death Row Lamb Tacos
	Grilled Black Pepper Crusted Whole Pork Tenderloin
	Smoky, Spicy Ribs with a Buzz
	Spicy Pulled Pork (Carnitas)
	Roasted Turkey Breast
	Melt Your Mouth Snapper over Jasmine Rice
	Marcie Gras Paella
	Sausage Stuffed Hot Peppers
Beer, Argentine	Argentine Style Grilled Whole Beef Tenderloin
Beer, Czech	Slovak Kapustnica
Beer, Italian	Mini Italian Sausages
	Sausage Stuffed Hot Peppers
Beer, German	Axis of Chicken Parmesan
Beer, Japanese	Black Pepper and Sesame Crusted Seared Tuna Sashimi
Beer, Mexican	Mini Shrimp Quesadillas
	Tequila Lime Shrimp

What To Swill	When you Grill
Beer, Mexican	Chicken Tortilla Soup
	Spicy Pulled Pork (Carnitas)
Beaujolais	Beef Tenderloin Tartare
Bloody Maria	Crispy Jalapeño Hash brown Frittata
Bloody Mary	Huevos al Bilito
	Shrimpanadas
	Salmon-Rye Breakfast Toast Strips
	Shaved Tenderloin Steak Sandwich Pita
Bloody Mary, Bar for	*Preparation instructions*
Bloody Mary, Recipe for	*Preparation instructions*
Bourbon Manhattan	Prosciutto and Gorgonzola Flank Steak Pinwheels
	Colossal Shrimp Thermador
Bouzo	Kalamata Olive Tapenade
Cabernet Sauvignon	Standing Rib Roast with New Potatoes
	Grilled Rack of Lamb
Chablis	Vera Cruz Red Snapper (Huachinango Veracruzana)
	Panko Crusted Pompano Filets
Chardonnay	Seafood Stuffed Mushrooms
	Shrimp 'n Crab Cakes
	Colossal Shrimp Thermador
Champagne/Sparkling White Wine	Strawberry-Papaya Salsa
	Tequila Lime Chicken Livers
	Butter and Parmesan Grilled Oysters
	Sweet and Savory Crepes
	Perfectly Poached Eggs Without Gadgets
	Benedict Allen
Chianti	Grilled Provoletta
	Axis of Chicken Parmesan
	Red Headed Red Sauce
	Sausage and Ricotta Stuffed Manicotti
	Crispy Eggplant Parmesan
	Sausage Stuffed Hot Peppers

What To Swill	When you Grill
Cosmopolitan, Fizzy Redneck	*Preparation instructions*
Greek, Cypriot, or Croatian White Wine	"Which came first, the Avgo or the Lemono?" (Greek Chicken Soup with Egg and Lemon)
Green Drink, The	*Preparation instructions*
Greyhound, Vodka	Rosemary Breakfast Potatoes Au Gratin
Malbec	Argentine Style Whole Grilled Beef Tenderloin
Martini, Chocolate	*Preparation instructions*
Martini, Olive Soup	*Preparation instructions*
Margaritas	Pico de Gallo Chicken Tortilla Soup Mahi Mahi Tacos
Merlot	Prosciutto and Gorgonzola Flank Steak Pinwheels
Mimosas	One Dish Breakfast Bake Perfectly Poached Eggs Without Gadgets Benedict Allen
Petit Sirah	Standing Rib Roast with New Potatoes
Pinot Blanc	Which came first, the Avgo or the Lemono Panko Crusted Pompano Filets
Pinot Grigio	Pluots and Gorgonzola Wrapped in Prosciutto Panko Crusted Pompano Filets Scallops in Beurre Blanc
Pinot Noir	Sausage Stuffed Mushrooms Seafood Stuffed Mushrooms Chicken Soup for the Belly Grilled Black Pepper Crusted Whole Pork Tenderloin Spicy Pulled Pork (Carnitas) Prosciutto and Swiss Cheese Stuffed Chicken Breasts Roasted Turkey Breast
Rioja	Cuban Sandwich Marcie Gras Paella

What To Swill	When you Grill
Sake	Black Pepper and Sesame Crusted Seared Tuna Sashimi
Sangiovese	Axis of Chicken Parmesan
	Red Headed Red Sauce
	Sausage and Ricotta Stuffed Manicotti
	Crispy Eggplant Parmesan
	Sausage Stuffed Hot Peppers
Sauvignon Blanc	Shrimp 'n Crab Cakes
	New England Seafood Chowder
	Prosciutto and Swiss Cheese Stuffed Chicken Breasts
	Lemon-Rosemary Roasted Chicken with Vegetables
	Crab and Shrimp Stuffed Tilapia
	Panko Crusted Pompano Filets
	Marcie Gras Paella
Super Tuscan	"Game Over" Stuffed Venison Tenderloin
	Mac and Cheese and Cheese and Cheese
	Sausage and Ricotta Stuffed Manicotti
Syrah/Shiraz	Standing Rib Roast with New Potatoes
	"Game Over" Stuffed Venison Tenderloin
	Goat Cheese-Tapenade Stuffed Lamb Chops
	Death Row Lamb Tacos
	Smoky, Spicy Ribs with a Buzz
Tempranillo	Argentine Style Whole Grilled Beef Tenderloin
Tequila	Guacamole
Viognier	Panko Crusted Pompano Filets
	Melt Your Mouth Snapper over Jasmine Rice
Vodka, Club Soda and	Shrimp 'n Crab Cakes
Zinfandel (Red)	Herb-Rubbed Boneless Leg of Lamb
	Goat Cheese-Tapenade Stuffed Lamb Chops
	Death Row Lamb Tacos

Acknowledgements

The author would like to thank the following people for their invaluable contribution to this project: Teri Watkins and Audrey Welch at Author House for enduring my seemingly endless stream of questions; Marlene Petrella for tirelessly editing this into something that I'm proud of; Sandy and Jordan for smiling through many years of experiments while their Dad learned how to cook; Brad Thompson for his motivational speeches and encouragement; Ken Hope for introducing me to "Greasy Pizza Guy Day"; Mom for letting me have free run of the kitchen; and to all of the friends and co-workers that survived the testing of these recipes over the years. Thanks to Bill Doonan, Steve Drege, and Judy Balas for teaching me to properly count olives; to Nick and Becky Giambrone, Mark Bolduc, and Steve Wyse for all of the creative marketing and cover ideas. Thanks to Zeus and Ally and Jan and Jim for trusting me with your daughter. Finally, thank you to Marcie, my best friend, my wife, and the one person who I can fully trust to let me know when I've made a lousy dinner.